BALLOON ART

By Marvin Hardy

BALLOON ART

For best results, balloons should be stored in plastic and should not be exposed to light and extremes of temperature.

ISBN: 0-934126-76-3

First Printing July 1985
Randall Book Co.
Salt Lake City, Utah

Printed in the United States of America
Typography by Executype

TABLE OF CONTENTS

FOREWORD

I became acquainted with Marvin Hardy several years ago through his magic shows at the county library, a local mall, and others. His fine reputation had preceded him. I sought out his shows, having heard ''rave reviews'' from other colleagues on the regional entertainment circuit. One mutual and dear performing friend, ''Trice'' Cartwright-Smith, story-teller extraordinaire (whom I had introduced to balloon twisting), subsequently introduced Marvin to the fascinating world of balloon art. Thus, I choose to claim a small indirect credit in the development of the world's foremost authority on balloon figures.

With his inate flair for creativity and showmanship evolved from years as a first-rate performing magician, Marvin took to balloon sculpture with characteristic enthusiasm and unprecedented productivity. He has simply blown the walls down that for years had defined the limits of the possible for balloon artists. The extraordinary detail and refinement of his one-balloon creations astonishes even veteran balloon sculptors. Not content to limit himself to simple balloon animals as most balloon entertainers do, his world of balloon figures includes flowers, planes, motorcycles, a light sabre, celebrity caricatures, and many more phenomenally-detailed one-balloon innovations.

Not one to jealously guard his secrets, Marvin has generously shared his expertise. He is just as quick to demonstrate advanced techniques to skilled colleagues as he is to freely teach basic twists to children and beginners.

Having written and published several smaller *Balloon Magic* books, Marvin went on to develop a unique balloon pump. Packaging the pump, an instructional book of top quality, and a supply of balloons, he began to make the fun of balloon figures available to the world with complete kits for novice to expert balloon sculptors.

Now, with the publication of *Balloon Art,* a truly authoritative presentation of balloon skills is being made available for the first time. But even this work is not definitive in the magical mind of Marvin Hardy. On his expanding horizon is a monumental, two-volume encyclopedia of balloonology. Yes, balloon-ology. Like the other -ologies of the worlds of science (biology, geology, etc.) Marvin is developing a ''science'' of balloon-working. Nevertheless, he would be the first to remind us that it's really more art than science. But in the dexterous hands of Marvin Hardy, balloons are even more than art—they are truly magic!

Gary D. Willden, Ed.D.
Assoc. Prof. of Recreation, Weber State College

a.k.a. Lupo t. Clown, Ph.D.
(Doctor of Phunology), Ogden, Utah

INFLATING

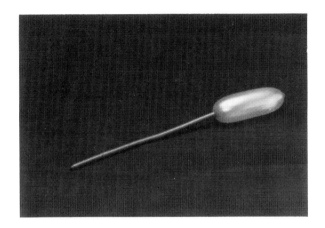

One of the most difficult things to learn in the creation of balloon figures is how much to inflate the balloon. A portion of the balloon must be left uninflated to allow for expansion of the air in the balloon. Each twist in the formation of a balloon figure forces a portion of the air towards the uninflated end of the balloon. It is fairly easy to adjust for too little air by simply changing the size of portions of the balloon figure, but it is impossible to complete a figure if there is too much air in the balloon. Only practice will teach you how much to inflate a balloon for each figure as no two people form the bubbles in exactly the same manner. As a general rule, however, leave approximately ½ inch of the balloon uninflated for each twist required to form the balloon figure you are working on. The natural tendency is to overinflate so start with less air than you think you will need until you have practiced enough to have confidence in your own judgment. Most figures can be formed with 6 inches to 8 inches of the balloon left uninflated.

TYING

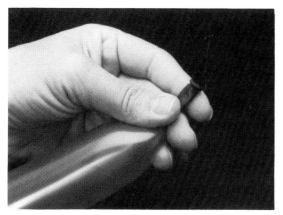

Many people find it difficult to tie a balloon. Although any method is acceptable, I find the simplest way is to grasp the end of the balloon between the thumb and the side of the first joint of the middle finger of the left hand with the rolled lip of the balloon extending upward.

Grasp the rolled lip of the balloon between the thumb and the first finger of the right hand. Stretch it out and wrap it clockwise around the ends of the first and middle fingers of the left hand.

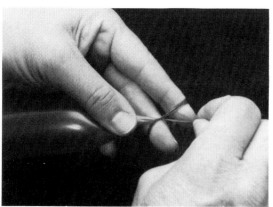

Tuck the rolled lip of the balloon down through the space between the first and middle fingers of the left hand. Grasp the rolled lip again after it passes behind the stretched out portion of the balloon and hold it while removing the left fingers from the loop that is formed.

BASIC TWISTS

There are several basic twists or formations of bubbles which are common to a variety of figures. These basic twists will be explained in detail preceding the series of figures to which they apply. If a twist has been explained earlier in the book, it will be referred to by page number but will not be explained again.

LOCK TWIST

Each series of bubbles must be held in place by a lock twist to prevent it from untwisting. A lock twist is formed by twisting together the base of two bubbles or the two ends of the same bubble.

TWO BUBBLE TWIST

Hold the inflated balloon in your left hand with the uninflated end pointing to your right. Form a bubble of the desired length. Double the balloon at the twist and form a second bubble equal in length to the first.

Lock twist these two bubbles at the base.

BASIC ANIMAL

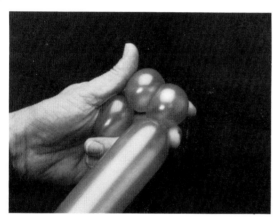

Inflate the balloon leaving an 8 inch uninflated end and tie a knot. Hold the balloon in your left hand with the uninflated end pointing to your right. Form a 1 inch bubble for the head followed by two 1 inch bubbles.

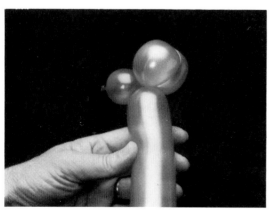

Lock twist the two 1 inch bubbles at the base to form the ears.

Form a 1 inch bubble for the neck followed by two 2 inch bubbles. Lock twist the two 2 inch bubbles at the base to form the front legs.

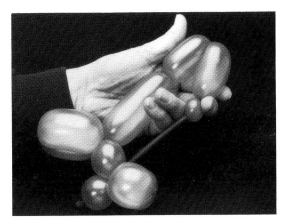

Form a 3 inch bubble for the body followed by two 2 inch bubbles. Lock twist the two 2 inch bubbles at the base to form the back legs. Be sure to leave a small bubble of air at the base of the tail to hold the back legs in place.

PROPORTION

It is a simple fact that most animals are basically similar. They each have a head, two ears, a neck, two front legs, a body, two back legs, and a tail. Any of the basic animal figures can be easily formed using the twists outlined in the previous figure by simply changing the proportion or relative size of a series of bubbles. A rabbit, for instance, has long ears, a short neck, short front legs, long back legs, and a short tail. A giraffe has short ears, a long neck, long front legs, shorter back legs and a long tail. A mouse is small in every detail. The same basic twists are used for each of these figures. The following six pages show the formation of these three figures.

MOUSE

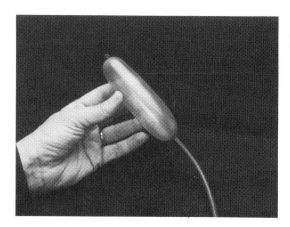

Inflate the balloon to form a 5 inch bubble and tie a knot.

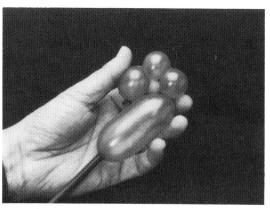

Hold the balloon in your left hand with the uninflated end pointing to your right. Form a 1 inch bubble for the head followed by two 1 inch bubbles. Lock twist the two 1 inch bubbles at the base to form the ears.

Form a ½ inch bubble for the neck followed by two 1 inch bubbles. Lock twist the two 1 inch bubbles at the base to form the front legs.

Form a 1 inch bubble for the body followed by two 1 inch bubbles. Lock twist the two 1 inch bubbles at the base to form the back legs. Be sure to leave a small bubble of air at the base of the tail to hold the back legs in place.

GIRAFFE

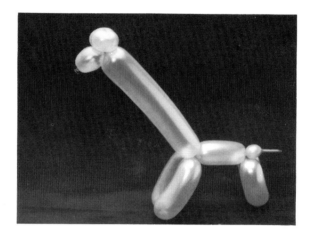

Inflate the balloon leaving a 4 inch uninflated end and tie a knot. Hold the balloon in your left hand with the uninflated end pointing to your right. Form a 1 inch bubble for the head followed by two 1 inch bubbles. Lock twist the two 1 inch bubbles at the base to form the ears.

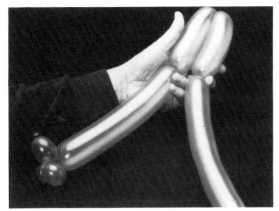

Form an 8 inch bubble for the neck followed by two 4 inch bubbles. Lock twist the two 4 inch bubbles at the base to form the front legs.

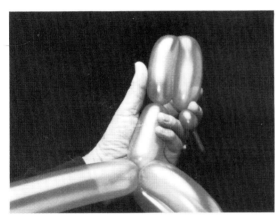

Form a 3 inch bubble for the body followed by two 3 inch bubbles. Lock twist the two 3 inch bubbles at the base to form the back legs. Be sure to leave a small bubble of air at the base of the tail to hold the back legs in place.

BUNNY RABBIT

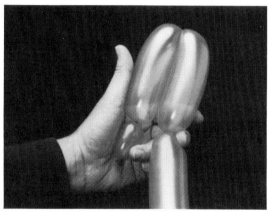

Inflate the balloon leaving a 3 inch uninflated end and tie a knot. Hold the balloon in your left hand with the uninflated end pointing to your right. Form a 1 inch bubble for the head followed by two 3 inch bubbles. Lock twist the two 3 inch bubbles at the base to form the ears.

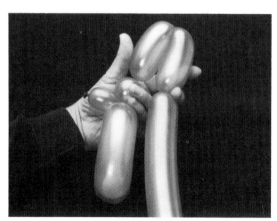

Form a 1 inch bubble for the neck followed by two 2 inch bubbles. Lock twist the two 2 inch bubbles at the base to form the front legs.

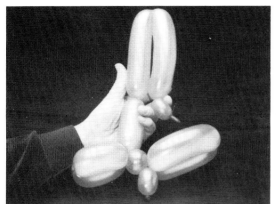

Form a 3 inch bubble for the body followed by two 4 inch bubbles. Lock twist the two 4 inch bubbles at the base to form the back legs. Be sure to leave a small bubble of air at the base of the tail to hold the back legs in place.

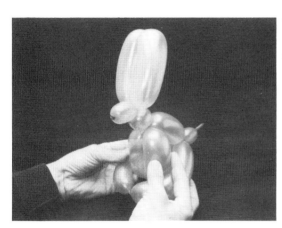

The front legs may be tucked between the back legs to place the figure in a sitting position.

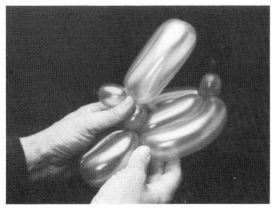

Wedge the body between the back legs with the front legs extended forward to place the figure in a laying position.

ADDING DETAIL

Several different animal figures can be easily and quickly formed using only the basic twists described on the preceding pages. To me, however, the real challenge in balloon art is to form figures showing detail that is unique to the figure being formed. The following pages describe a variety of twists or formations of bubbles which add specific characteristics to the figure being formed.

FLOPPY EARS

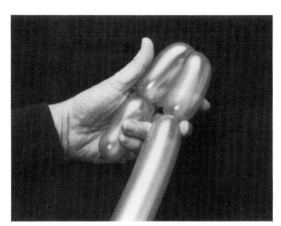

Hold the inflated balloon in your left hand with the uninflated end pointing to your right. Form a 2 inch bubble for the head followed by two 2 inch bubbles. Lock twist the two 2 inch bubbles at the base to form the ears.

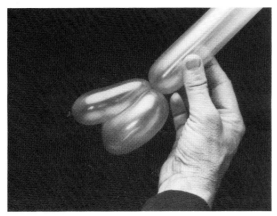

Turn the balloon so that the ears are pointing downward. Wedge the bubble which forms the head between the two ears so that it also points downward.

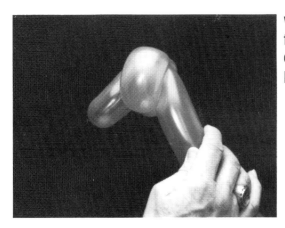

Wedge the inflated portion of the balloon between the ears opposite the head so that it also points downward.

Forming the head in this way gives the appearance of long floppy ears which are common to many animal figures. The following two figures are examples of this characteristic.

BASSETT HOUND

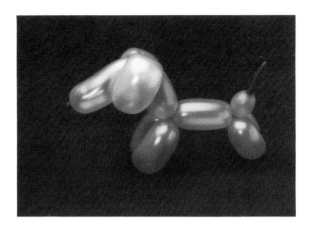

Inflate the balloon leaving a 6 inch uninflated end and tie a knot. Hold the balloon in your left hand with the uninflated end pointing to your right. Form a 2 inch bubble for the head followed by two 2 inch bubbles. Lock twist the second and third 2 inch bubbles at the base to form the ears.

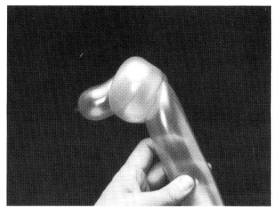

Turn the balloon so that the ears are pointing downward. Wedge the head and neck bubbles between the ears so that they both point downward to complete the head.

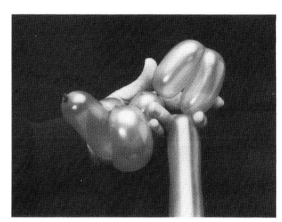

Form a 2 inch bubble for the neck followed by two 2 inch bubbles. Lock twist the second and third 2 inch bubbles at the base to form the front legs.

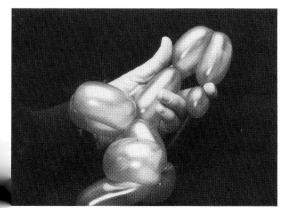

Form a 3 inch bubble for the body followed by two 2 inch bubbles. Lock twist the two 2 inch bubbles at the base to form the back legs. Be sure to leave a small bubble of air at the base of the tail to hold the back legs in place.

DACHSHUND

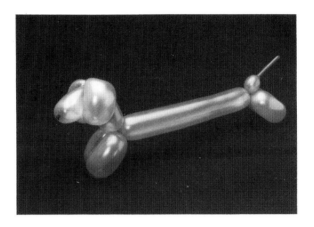

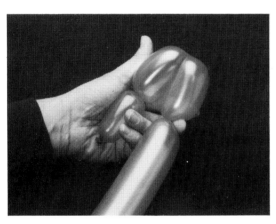

Inflate the balloon leaving a 6 inch uninflated end and tie a knot. Hold the balloon in your left hand with the uninflated end pointing to your right. Form a 1½ inch bubble for the head followed by two 1½ inch bubbles. Lock twist the second and third 1½ inch bubbles at the base to form the ears.

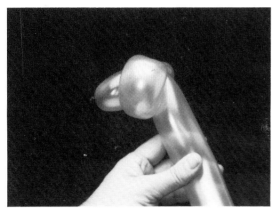

Turn the balloon so that the ears are pointing downward. Wedge the head and neck bubbles between the ears so that they both point downward to complete the head.

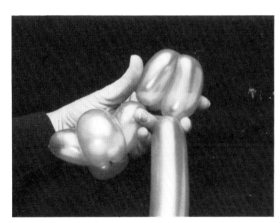

Form a 1½ inch bubble for the neck followed by two 1½ inch bubbles. Lock twist the second and third 1½ inch bubbles at the base to form the front legs.

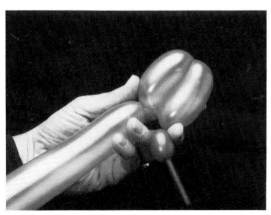

Form an 8 inch bubble for the body followed by two 1½ inch bubbles. Lock twist the two 1½ inch bubbles at the base to form the back legs. Be sure to leave a small bubble of air at the base of the tail to hold the back legs in place.

LOOP TWIST

The loop twist is used to form simple ears and legs, the petals of flowers, the back legs of animals which stand erect such as the bear, the feet of some birds, the hand guards of the sword, and the wings and rudders of airplanes.

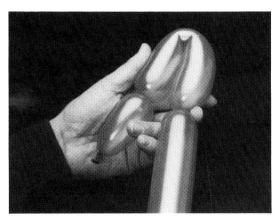

Hold the inflated balloon in your left hand with the uninflated end of the balloon pointing to your right. Double the balloon from the point of the last twist to form the size of loop that is desired. For the purpose of the instructions in this book, the size of loop is measured from the twist at the base of the loop to the outer edge of the loop.

Twist the balloon at the end of the loop at a point where both sides of the loop are equal. Lock twist the two ends of the loop together.

BASIC LOOP FIGURE

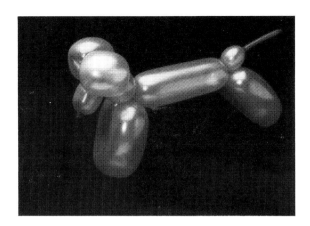

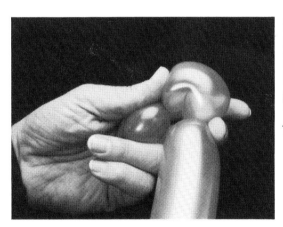

Inflate the balloon leaving an 8 inch uninflated end and tie a knot. Hold the balloon in your left hand with the uninflated end pointing to your right. Form a 1 inch bubble for the head followed by a 1 inch loop.

Lock twist the ends of this loop to form one ear.

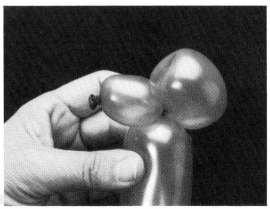

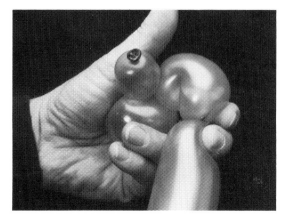

Form a second 1 inch loop. Lock twist the ends of this loop to form the other ear.

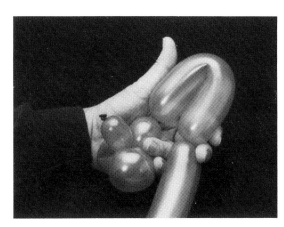

Form a 1 inch bubble for the neck followed by a 4 inch loop. Lock twist the ends of this loop to form the front legs.

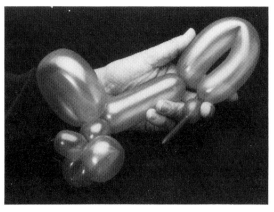

Form a 4 inch bubble for the body followed by another 4 inch loop. Lock twist the ends of this loop to form the back legs. Be sure to leave a small bubble of air at the base of the tail to hold the back legs in place.

CAT

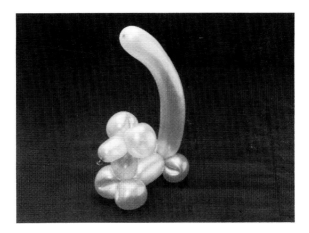

Inflate the balloon leaving a 6 inch uninflated end and tie a knot. Hold the balloon in your left hand with the uninflated end pointing to your right. Form a 1 inch bubble for the head followed by a 1 inch loop.

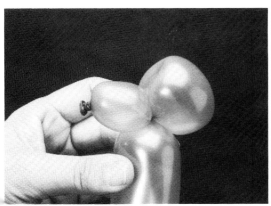

Lock twist the ends of this loop to form one ear.

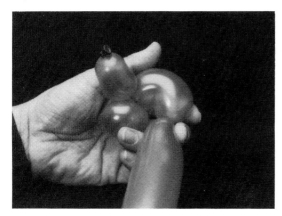

Form a second 1 inch loop. Lock twist the ends of this loop to form the other ear.

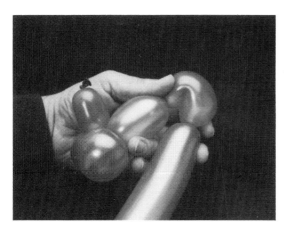

Form a 1½ inch bubble for the body followed by a 1 inch loop. Lock twist the ends of this loop to form one front leg.

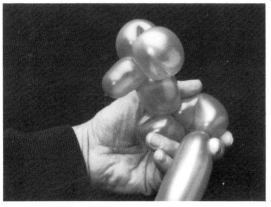

Form a second 1 inch loop. Lock twist the ends of this loop to form the other front leg.

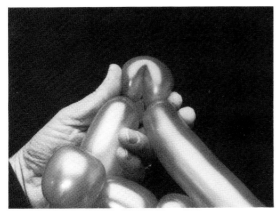

Form a 3 inch bubble for the body followed by a 1 inch loop. Lock twist the ends of this loop to form one back leg.

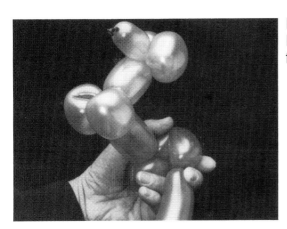

Form a second 1 inch loop. Lock twist the ends of this loop to form the other back leg.

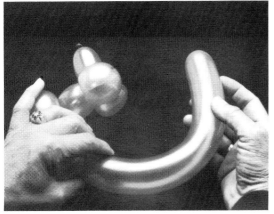

Curve the tail up over the body to complete the figure.

LOOP AND TUCK

The loop and tuck is used for the head of some animal figures, the wheels of some vehicles, the tails of some birds, and the head of the doll. It can be formed in two ways. First, with a small bubble forming the center of a loop, and second, with a long bubble passing through a loop.

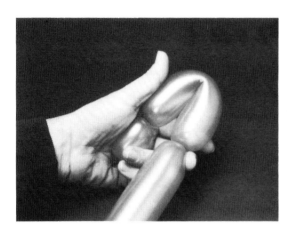

Hold the inflated balloon in your left hand with the uninflated end pointing to your right. Form a 1 inch bubble followed by a 1½ inch loop. Lock twist the two ends of the loop at the base.

Tuck the 1 inch bubble inside the center of the loop.

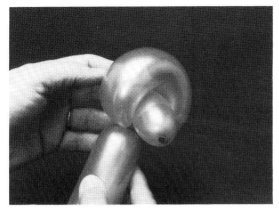

Hold the inflated balloon in your left hand with the uninflated end pointing to your right. Form a 3 inch bubble followed by a 1½ inch loop. Lock twist the two ends of the loop at the base. Tuck half of the 3 inch bubble through the center of the loop.

FOUR BUBBLE TWIST

The four bubble twist is used to add detail to the legs of several figures.

Hold the balloon in your left hand with the uninflated end pointing to your right. Form a 2 inch bubble followed by a 1 inch bubble, two ½ inch bubbles, and another 1 inch bubble.

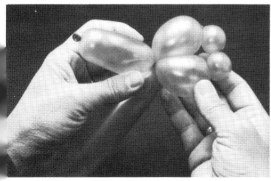

Lock twist the two 1 inch bubbles at the base to form a four bubble leg assembly.

The following three animal figures show examples of loop and tuck ears and the four bubble leg assembly.

MONKEY

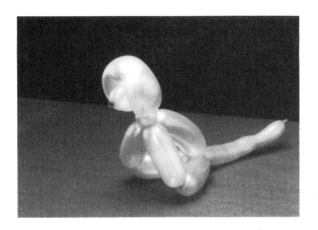

Inflate the balloon leaving a 6 inch uninflated end and tie a knot. Hold the balloon in your left hand with the uninflated end pointing to your right. Form a 1½ inch bubble for the head followed by a 2 inch loop. Lock twist the ends of this loop.

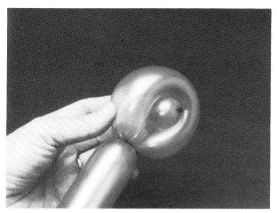

Roll the knot end of the 1½ inch bubble through the center of the 2 inch loop to complete the head.

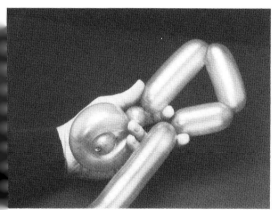

Form a 1 inch bubble for the neck followed by a 4 inch bubble and two 3 inch bubbles. Lock twist the 4 inch bubble and the second 3 inch bubble at the base to form the back and legs on one side.

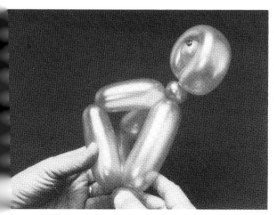

Form two 3 inch bubbles. Lock twist the base of the second 3 inch bubble around the base of the 4 inch bubble which was formed in Step 3 to complete the figure.

POODLE

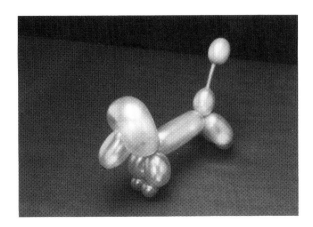

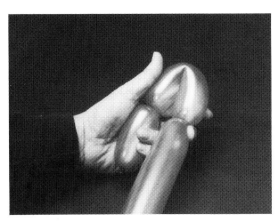

Inflate the balloon leaving an 8 inch uninflated end and tie a knot. Hold the balloon in your left hand with the uninflated end pointing to your right. Form a 3 inch bubble followed by a 1½ inch loop. Lock twist the two ends of this loop to form the head.

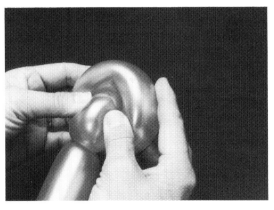

Tuck half of the 3 inch bubble through the center of the 1½ inch loop to complete the head.

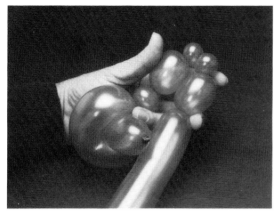

Form a 1 inch bubble for the neck followed by a 1½ inch bubble, two ½ inch bubbles, and another 1½ inch bubble. Lock twist the two 1½ inch bubbles at the base to form the front legs.

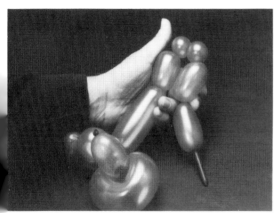

Form a 3 inch bubble for the body followed by a 1½ bubble, two ½ inch bubbles, and another 1½ inch bubble. Lock twist the two 1½ inch bubbles at the base to form the back legs.

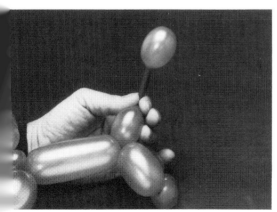

Form a 1 inch bubble at the base of the tail. Force the remainder of the air in the balloon to the end of the uninflated tip to form a ball at the end of the tail and complete the figure.

PINCH TWIST

The pinch twist is used to form the ears of several animal figures, to give shape to a series of bubbles, and to hold bubbles in place.

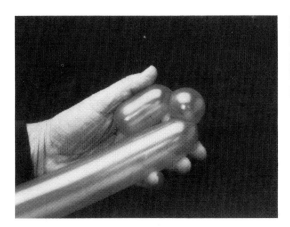

Hold the balloon in your left hand with the uninflated end pointing to your right. Form a 3 inch bubble followed by a 1 inch bubble.

Grasp the sides of this 1 inch bubble with the thumb and first finger of your right hand. Stretch this bubble out while pinching the two ends of the bubble firmly together with the thumb and first finger of your left hand.

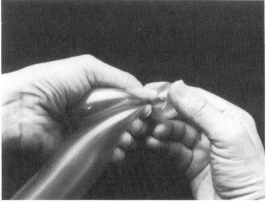

Twist the pinched bubble three or more times with the right hand.

THREE BUBBLE WITH PINCH

The three bubble with pinch is used to form the head and ears of several different animal figures.

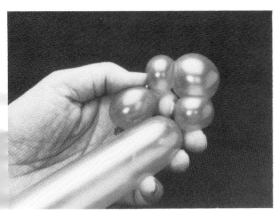

Hold the inflated balloon in your left hand with the uninflated end pointing to your right. Form a 1 inch bubble followed by a ½ inch bubble, a 1 inch bubble, and another ½ inch bubble. Lock twist the two ½ inch bubbles at the base to form the head.

Pinch twist the two ½ inch bubbles to form the ears and complete the head.

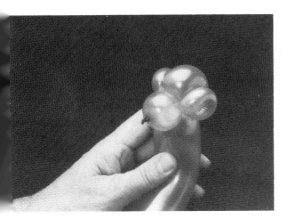

CHIHUAHUA

Inflate the balloon to form a 6 inch bubble and tie a knot. Hold the balloon in your left hand with the uninflated end pointing to your right. Form a 1 inch bubble for the head followed by a ½ inch bubble, a 1 inch bubble, and another ½ inch bubble. Lock twist the two ½ inch bubbles at the base to complete the head.

Pinch twist the first ½ inch bubble to form one ear.

Pinch twist the second ½ inch bubble to form the other ear.

Form a 1 inch bubble for the neck followed by two 1 inch bubbles. Lock twist the two 1 inch bubbles at the base to form the front legs.

Form a 2 inch bubble for the body followed by two 1 inch bubbles. Lock twist the two 1 inch bubbles at the base to form the back legs. Be sure to leave a small bubble of air at the base of the tail to hold the back legs in place.

POODLE WITH EARS

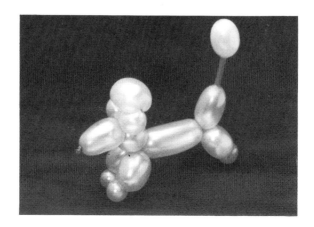

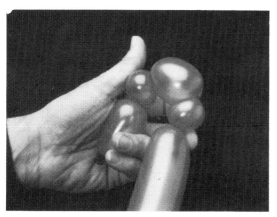

Inflate the balloon leaving an 8 inch uninflated end and tie a knot. Hold the balloon in your left hand with the uninflated end pointing to your right. Form a 1 inch bubble for the head followed by a ½ inch bubble, a 1½ inch bubble, and another ½ inch bubble.

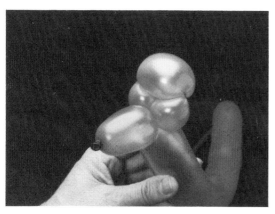

Lock twist the two ½ inch bubbles at the base to form the head.

Form a 1 inch bubble for the neck followed by a 1½ inch bubble, two ½ inch bubbles, and another 1½ inch bubble. Lock twist the two 1½ inch bubbles at the base to form the front legs.

Form a 3 inch bubble for the body followed by a 1½ inch bubble, two ½ inch bubbles, and another 1½ inch bubble. Lock twist the two 1½ inch bubbles at the base to form the back legs.

Form a 1 inch bubble at the base of the tail. Force the remainder of the air in the inflated portion of the balloon to the end of the uninflated portion of the balloon to form a ball at the end of the tail.

SQUIRREL

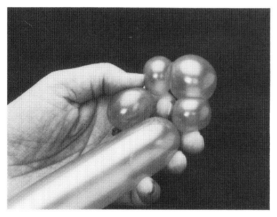

Inflate the balloon leaving a 6 inch uninflated end and tie a knot. Hold the balloon in your left hand with the uninflated end pointing to your right. Form a 1 inch bubble for the head followed by a ½ inch bubble, a 1 inch bubble, and another ½ inch bubble. Lock twist the two ½ inch bubbles at the base to form the head.

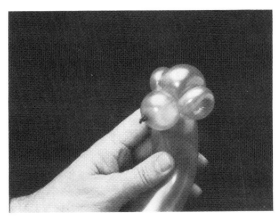

Pinch twist the two ½ inch bubbles to complete the ears.

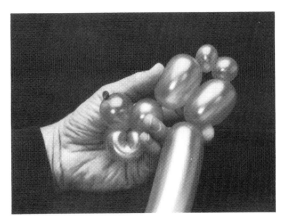

Form a 1 inch bubble for the neck followed by a 1½ inch bubble, two ½ inch bubbles, and another 1½ inch bubble. Lock twist the two 1½ inch bubbles at the base to form the front legs.

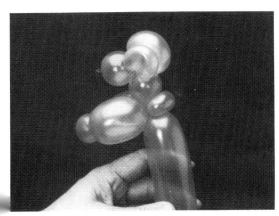

Form a 1 inch bubble. Pinch twist this bubble at the point where the front legs and the neck join to hold the head forward.

Form a 3 inch bubble for the body followed by a 2 inch loop. Lock twist the ends of this loop to form one back leg.

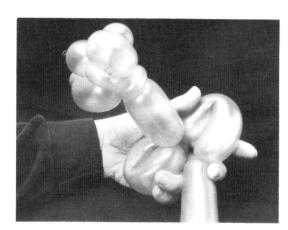

Form a 2 inch loop. Lock twist the ends of this loop to form the other back leg. Curve the tail up behind the body to complete the figure.

KANGAROO

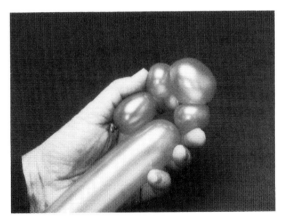

Inflate the balloon leaving a 6 inch uninflated end and tie a knot. Hold the balloon in your left hand with the uninflated end pointing to your right. Form a 1 inch bubble for the head followed by a ½ inch bubble, a 1 inch bubble, and another ½ inch bubble. Lock twist the two ½ inch bubbles at the base to complete the head.

Pinch twist the two ½ inch bubbles to form the ears.

Form a 1 inch bubble for the neck followed by a 1½ inch bubble, two ½ inch bubbles, and another 1½ inch bubble. Lock twist the two 1½ inch bubbles at the base to form the front legs.

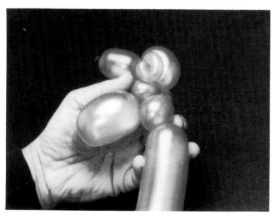

Form a 1 inch bubble at the base of the front legs.

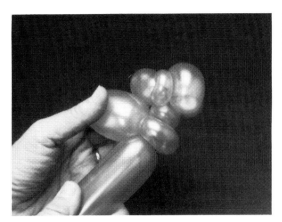

Pinch twist the 1 inch bubble behind the point where the front legs and the neck join to hold the head forward.

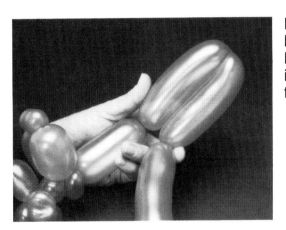

Form a 3 inch bubble for the body followed by two 4 inch bubbles. Lock twist the two 4 inch bubbles at the base to form the back legs.

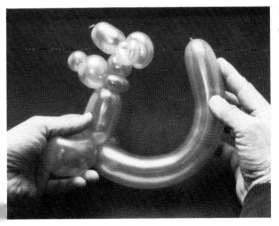

Curve the tail slightly upward to complete the figure.

ANTLERS

By adding bubbles to a standard two bubble ear assembly, antlers can be formed.

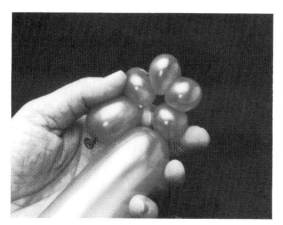

Hold the balloon in your left hand with the uninflated end pointing to your right. Form a 1 inch bubble followed by four ½ inch bubbles. Lock twist the first and fourth ½ inch bubbles at the base to form one side of the antlers.

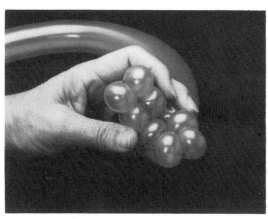

Form four ½ inch bubbles. Lock twist the first and fourth ½ inch bubbles at the base to form the other side of the antlers.

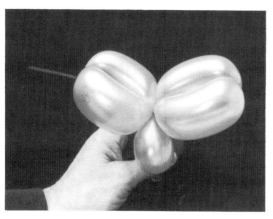

By using two 1½ inch bubbles instead of four ½ inch bubbles, the broad antlers of a moose can be formed.

The following animal figures show the use of several different kinds of antlers and horns.

DEER

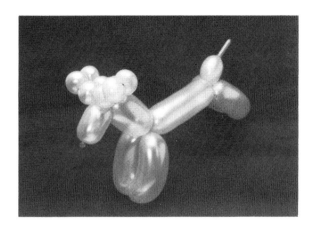

Inflate the balloon leaving an 8 inch uninflated end and tie a knot. Hold the balloon in your left hand with the uninflated end pointing to your right. Form a 1 inch bubble for the head followed by four ½ inch bubbles. Lock twist the first and fourth ½ inch bubbles at the base to form one side of the antlers.

Form four ½ inch bubbles. Lock twist the first and fourth ½ inch bubbles at the base to form the other side of the antlers.

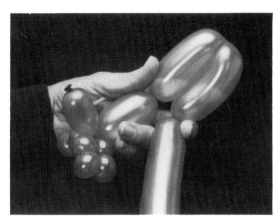

Form a 2 inch bubble for the neck followed by two 3 inch bubbles. Lock twist the two 3 inch bubbles at the base to form the front legs.

Form a 3 inch bubble for the body followed by two 3 inch bubbles. Lock twist the two 3 inch bubbles at the base to form the back legs. Be sure to leave a small bubble of air at the base of the tail to hold the back legs in place.

MOOSE

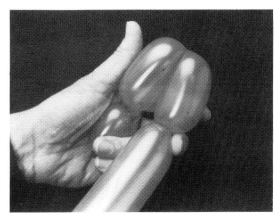

Inflate the balloon leaving a 6 inch uninflated end and tie a knot. Hold the balloon in your left hand with the uninflated end pointing to your right. Form a 1 inch bubble for the head followed by two 1½ inch bubbles. Lock twist the two 1½ inch bubbles at the base to form one side of the antlers.

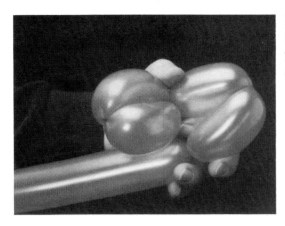

Form two 1½ inch bubbles. Lock twist these two bubbles at the base to form the other side of the antlers.

Form a 2 inch bubble for the neck followed by two 2 inch bubbles. Lock twist the two 2 inch bubbles at the base to form the front legs.

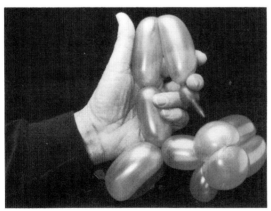

Form a 3 inch bubble for the body followed by two 2 inch bubbles. Lock twist the two 2 inch bubbles at the base to form the back legs. Be sure to leave a small bubble of air at the base of the tail to hold the back legs in place.

ELK

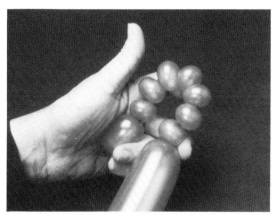

Inflate the balloon leaving an 8 inch uninflated end and tie a knot. Hold the balloon in your left hand with the uninflated end pointing to your right. Form a 1 inch bubble for the head followed by a chain of seven ½ inch bubbles.

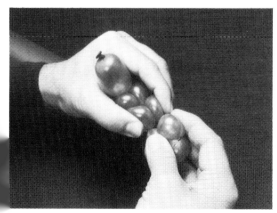

Lock twist the first and seventh ½ inch bubbles at the base to form a loop. Lock twist the third and fifth ½ inch bubbles to complete one side of the antlers.

Form a second chain of seven ½ inch bubbles. Lock twist the first and seventh ½ inch bubbles at the base. Lock twist the third and fifth ½ inch bubbles to complete the other side of the antlers.

Form a 2 inch bubble for the neck followed by two 3 inch bubbles. Lock twist the two 3 inch bubbles at the base to form the front legs.

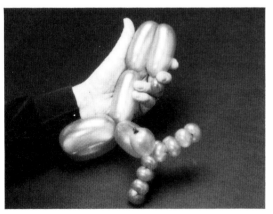

Form a 3 inch bubble for the body followed by two 3 inch bubbles. Lock twist the two 3 inch bubbles at the base to form the back legs. Be sure to leave a small bubble of air at the base of the tail to hold the back legs in place.

RAM/BIGHORN SHEEP

Inflate the balloon leaving a 6 inch uninflated end and tie a knot. Hold the balloon in your left hand with the uninflated end pointing to your right. Form a 1 inch bubble for the head followed by two 1 inch bubbles. Lock twist these two 1 inch bubbles at the base.

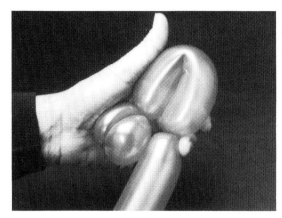

Form a 1½ inch loop. Lock twist the two ends of this loop to form one horn.

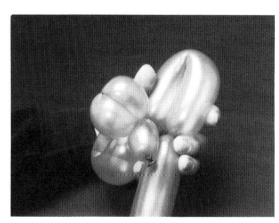

Form a second 1½ inch loop. Lock twist the two ends of this loop to form the other horn.

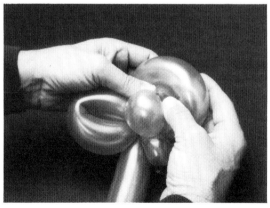

Tuck one of the 1 inch bubbles formed in step one into the center of one of the 1½ inch loops to complete one horn.

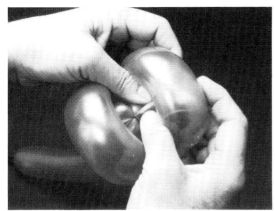

Tuck the other 1 inch bubble formed in step one into the center of the other 1 ½ inch loop to complete the other horn.

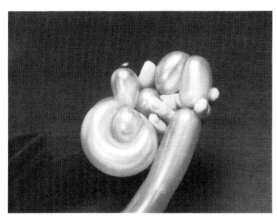

Form a 1 inch bubble for the neck followed by two 1 inch bubbles. Lock twist the two 1 inch bubbles at the base to form the front legs.

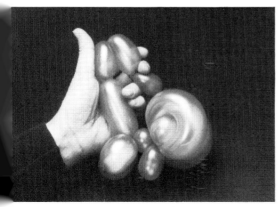

Form a 2 inch bubble for the body followed by two 1 inch bubbles. Lock twist the two 1 inch bubbles at the base to form the back legs. Be sure to leave a small bubble of air at the base of the tail to hold the back legs in place.

MANE

By adding a chain of small bubbles at the base of the neck and stretching this chain over the ears, the mane of the horse and unicorn can be formed.

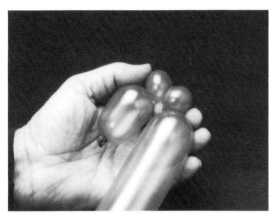

Hold the inflated balloon in your left hand with the uninflated end pointing to your right. Form a 1 inch bubble for the head followed by two ½ inch bubbles. Lock twist the two ½ inch bubbles at the base to form the ears.

Form a 1½ inch bubble for the neck followed by a chain of six ½ inch bubbles. Lock twist the first and sixth ½ inch bubbles at the base to form a loop.

Stretch the loop of six ½ inch bubbles over the ears wedging the ears between the third and fourth ½ inch bubbles to complete the mane.

HORSE

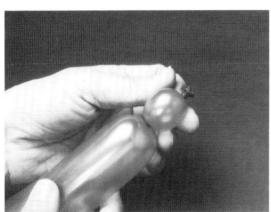

Inflate the balloon leaving an 8 inch uninflated end and tie a knot. Hold the balloon in your left hand with the uninflated end pointing to your right. Form a soft 1 inch bubble at the knot end of the balloon.

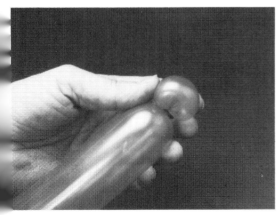

Pinch twist the 1 inch bubble.

Twist the pinch twisted bubble in half twisting each half three or four times to form the mouth.

Form a 1 inch bubble for the head followed by two ½ inch bubbles. Lock twist the two ½ inch bubbles at the base to form the ears.

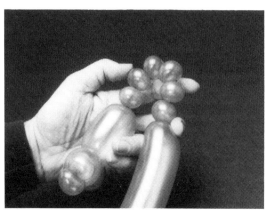

Form a 2 inch bubble for the neck followed by a chain of six ½ inch bubbles. Lock twist the first and sixth ½ inch bubbles at the base to form a loop.

Stretch the loop of six ½ inch bubbles over the ears wedging the ears between the third and fourth ½ inch bubbles to form the mane.

Form two 2 inch bubbles. Lock twist these two bubbles at the base to form the front legs.

Form a 3 inch bubble for the body followed by two 2 inch bubbles. Lock twist the two 2 inch bubbles at the base to form the back legs. Be sure to leave a small bubble of air at the base of the tail to hold the back legs in place.

ROCKING HORSE

Inflate the balloon leaving an 8 inch uninflated end and tie a knot. Hold the balloon in your left hand with the uninflated end pointing to your right. Form a soft 1 inch bubble at the knot end of the balloon.

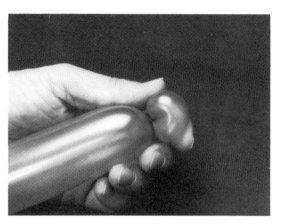

Pinch twist the 1 inch bubble.

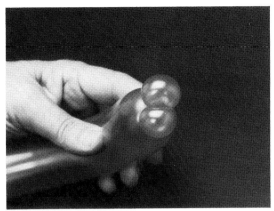

Twist the pinch twisted bubble in half twisting each half three or four times to form the mouth.

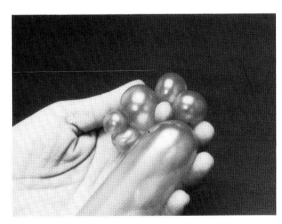

Form a ¾ inch bubble for the head followed by two ½ inch bubbles. Lock twist the two ½ inch bubbles at the base to form the ears.

Form a 1 inch bubble for the neck followed by four ½ inch bubbles. Lock twist the first and fourth ½ inch bubbles at the base to form a loop.

Stretch the loop of four ½ inch bubbles over the ears wedging the ears between the second and third ½ inch bubbles to form the mane.

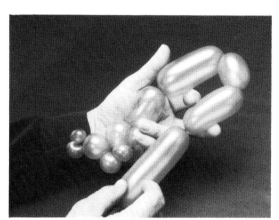

Form a 2 inch bubble for the front leg followed by a 3 inch bubble for the rocker, a 2 inch bubble for the back leg, and another 2 inch bubble for the back. Lock twist the first and third 2 inch bubbles at the base to complete one side.

Form a 2 inch bubble for the other front leg followed by a 3 inch bubble for the rocker and a 2 inch bubble for the back leg. Lock twist the second 2 inch bubble around the point where the back leg and the back join. Be sure to leave a small bubble of air at the base of the tail to hold the back legs in place.

By forming the chain of bubbles at the top of the neck instead of the base, the mane of the lion can be formed.

LION

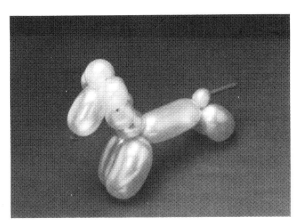

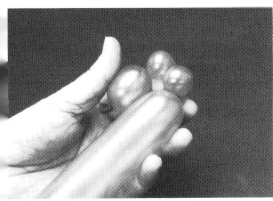

Inflate the balloon leaving an 8 inch uninflated end and tie a knot. Hold the balloon in your left hand with the uninflated end pointing to your right. Form a 1½ inch bubble for the head followed by two ½ inch bubbles.

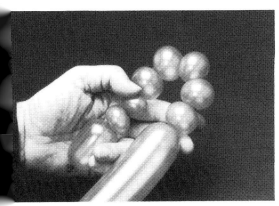

Hold the three bubbles formed in your left hand to prevent them from untwisting. Form a chain of five ¾ inch bubbles. Lock twist the first and fifth ¾ inch bubbles at the base to form a loop.

Tuck the 1½ inch bubble formed in Step 1 through the loop of ¾ inch bubbles to complete the head and mane.

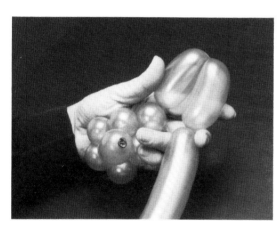

Form a 1 inch bubble for the neck followed by two 1½ inch bubbles. Lock twist the two 1½ inch bubbles at the base to form the front legs.

Form a 3 inch bubble for the body followed by two 1½ inch bubbles. Lock twist the two 1½ inch bubbles at the base to form the back legs. Be sure to leave a small bubble of air at the base of the tail to hold the back legs in place.

LAMB

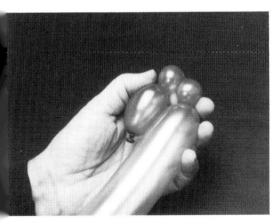

Inflate the balloon leaving an 8 inch uninflated end and tie a knot. Hold the balloon in your left hand with the uninflated end pointing to your right. Form a 1 inch bubble for the head followed by two ½ inch bubbles. Lock twist the two ½ inch bubbles at the base to form the ears.

Form a chain of seven ½ inch bubbles. Lock twist the third and seventh ½ inch bubbles at the base to form a five bubble loop.

Tuck the head and ears through the five bubble loop to complete the head.

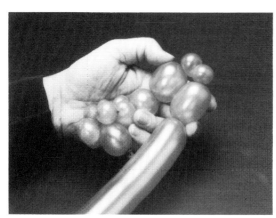

Form a 1 inch bubble for the neck followed by a 1½ inch bubble, two ½ inch bubbles, and another 1½ inch bubble. Lock twist the second and third 1½ inch bubbles at the base to form the front legs.

Form a 2 inch bubble for the body followed by a 1½ inch bubble, two ½ inch bubbles, and another 1½ inch bubble. Lock twist the two 1½ inch bubbles at the base to form the back legs. Be sure to leave a small bubble of air at the base of the tail to hold the back legs in place.

FIVE BUBBLE LOOP WITH PINCH TWIST

A five bubble loop with pinch twist is used to form the head of several figures such as the teddy bear.

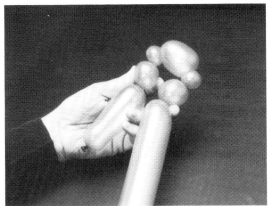

Hold the inflated balloon in your left hand with the uninflated balloon pointing to your right. Form a 3 inch bubble followed by a 1 inch bubble, a ½ inch bubble, a 1½ inch bubble, a ½ inch bubble, and another 1 inch bubble. Lock twist the two 1 inch bubbles at the base to form a five bubble loop.

Form a 2 inch bubble at the knot end of the 3 inch bubble formed in step one.

Tuck this 2 inch bubble through the center of the five bubble loop.

Pinch twist the two ½ inch bubbles to form the ears and complete the head.

FIVE BUBBLE LOOP WITH PINCH AND POP

The five bubble loop with pinch and pop is used to form the arms and legs of some figures, handlebars, wings and elevators of airplanes, and parts of other figures when it is desired to separate two sections of the balloon.

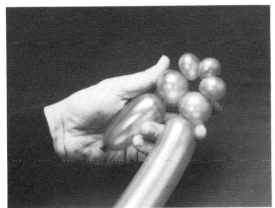

Hold the inflated balloon in your left hand with the uninflated end pointing to your right. Form a 2 inch bubble followed by a 1 inch bubble, three ½ inch bubbles, and another 1 inch bubble. Lock twist the two 1 inch bubbles at the base to form a 5 bubble loop.

Pinch twist the first and third ½ inch bubbles twisting each at least four times.

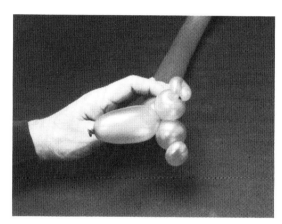

Pop the second ½ inch bubble to separate the pinch twisted bubbles.

TEDDY BEAR

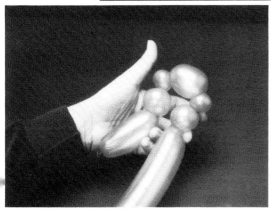

Inflate the balloon leaving a 6 inch uninflated end and tie a knot. Hold the balloon in your left hand with the uninflated end pointing to your right. Squeeze a small amount of air from the knot end of the balloon and form a soft 3 inch bubble followed by a 1 inch bubble, a ½ inch bubble, a 1½ inch bubble, a ½ inch bubble, and another 1 inch bubble. Lock twist the two 1 inch bubbles at the base to form a five bubble loop.

Form a 2 inch bubble at the knot end of the soft 3 inch bubble.

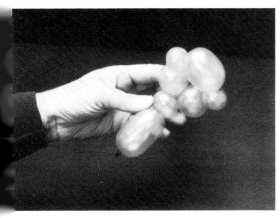

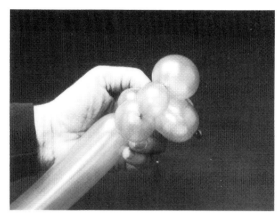

Tuck this 2 inch bubble through the center of the five bubble loop.

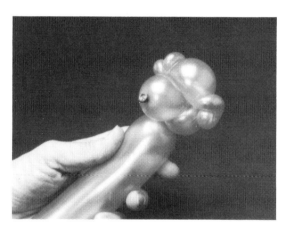

Pinch twist the two ½ inch bubbles of the five bubble loop to form the ears.

Form a 1 inch bubble for the neck followed by a 1½ inch bubble, three ½ inch bubbles, and another 1½ inch bubble. Lock twist the two 1½ inch bubbles at the base to form the front legs.

Pinch twist the first and third ½ inch bubbles twisting each at least four times. Pop the second ½ inch bubble to separate the front legs.

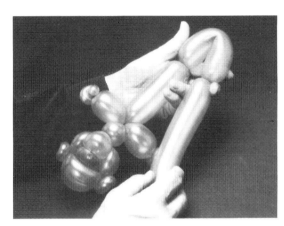

Form a 4 inch bubble for the body followed by a 2 inch loop. Lock twist the two ends of this loop to form one back leg.

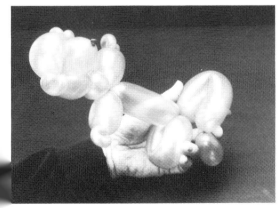

Form a second 2 inch loop. Lock twist the two ends of this loop to form the other back leg. Be sure to leave a small bubble of air at the base of the tail to hold the back legs in place.

TEDDY BEAR ON A UNICYCLE

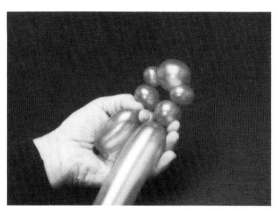

Inflate the balloon leaving an 8 inch uninflated end and tie a knot. Hold the balloon in your left hand with the uninflated end pointing to your right. Squeeze a small amount of air from the knot end of the balloon and form a soft 2½ inch bubble followed by a ¾ inch bubble, a ½ inch bubble, a 1 inch bubble, another ½ inch bubble, and another ¾ inch bubble.

Lock twist the two ¾ inch bubbles at the base to form a 5 bubble loop.

Form a 1½ inch bubble at the knot end of the soft 2½ inch bubble formed in Step 1. Tuck this 2 inch bubble through the center of the five bubble loop.

Pinch twist the two ½ inch bubbles of the five bubble loop to form the ears and complete the head.

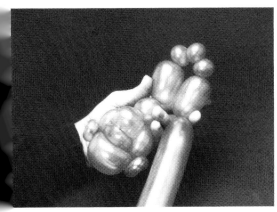

Form a ¾ inch bubble for the neck followed by a 1 inch bubble, three ½ inch bubbles, and another 1 inch bubble. Lock twist the two 1 inch bubbles at the base to form the front legs.

Pinch twist the first and third ½ inch bubbles twisting each at least four times. Pop the second ½ inch bubble to separate the front legs.

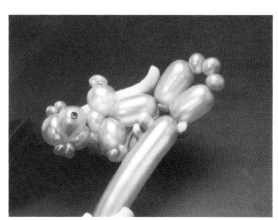

Form a 2 inch bubble for the body followed by a 1½ inch bubble, three ½ inch bubbles, and another 1½ inch bubble. Lock twist the two 1½ inch bubbles at the base to form the back legs.

Form a ½ inch bubble at the tip of the remaining portion of the balloon. Wrap the remaining portion of the balloon around the back legs so that one back leg is on each side of the loop that is formed. Lock twist the ½ inch bubble at the tip of the balloon around the point where the back legs and the body join to complete the figure.

TULIP TWIST

The Tulip Twist is used to form the tulip from which it gets its name. It is also used to form the center of other flowers, the propeller or jet engine of airplanes, and to add detail to the ends of several figures such as the sword and the pistol.

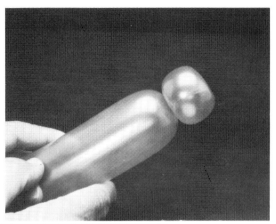

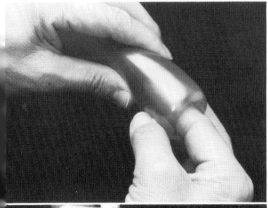

Hold the inflated balloon in your left hand with the knot end pointing to your right and the uninflated end pointing to your left. With the end of the first finger of your right hand, push the knot down inside of the balloon to whatever depth is desired for the tulip twist being formed.

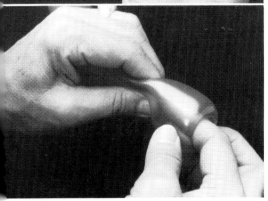

With the thumb and first finger of your left hand, pinch the sides of the balloon and grasp the knot inside of the balloon. Carefully remove the first finger of your right hand from the balloon while holding the knot firmly inside of the balloon with your left hand.

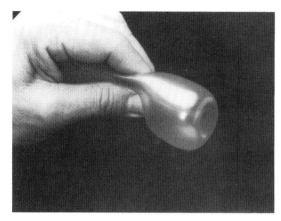

Twist the balloon three or more times with your right hand at the point where it is being held by the left hand.

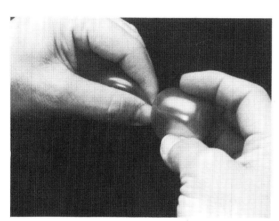

While holding the bubble with your right hand release the knot with your left hand and push it slightly into the base of the bubble before releasing the bubble with your right hand.

TULIP

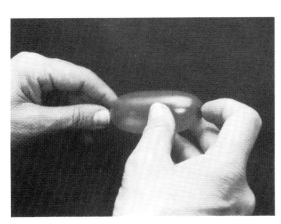

Inflate the balloon to form a 2 inch bubble and tie a knot. Hold the uninflated end of the balloon firmly at the base of the bubble with the thumb and first finger of your left hand.

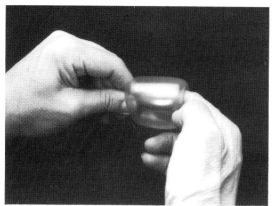

With the end of the first finger of your right hand, push the knot all the way through the bubble and grasp it between the thumb and first finger of your left hand without allowing any air to escape from the bubble.

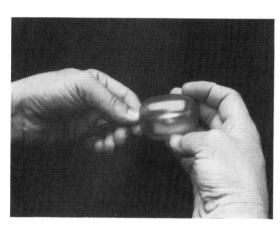

While holding the knot firmly with your left hand twist the bubble three or more times with your right hand.

Release the knot with your left hand and push it slightly into the base of the bubble before releasing the bubble with your right hand.

DAISY

Inflate the balloon to form a 3 inch bubble and tie a knot. Hold the bubble in your left hand with the uninflated end pointing to your right. Form a ½ inch tulip twist at the knot end of the balloon followed by two ½ inch bubbles.

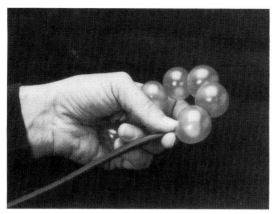

Hold the tulip twist and the two ½ inch bubbles in your left hand with the uninflated end pointing to your right. Form a chain of five ¾ inch bubbles.

Lock twist the first and fifth ¾ inch bubbles at the base to form a loop.

Tuck the tulip twist through the loop to form the center of the blossom.

ORCHID

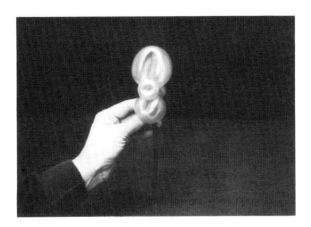

Inflate the balloon to form an 8 inch bubble and tie a knot. Hold the balloon in your left hand with the uninflated end pointing to your left. Form a 1 inch tulip twist at the knot end of the balloon.

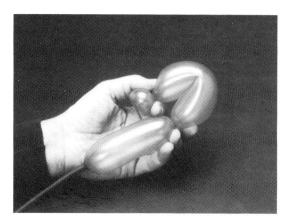

Form a 1½ inch loop. Lock twist the two ends of this loop to form the top portion of the blossom.

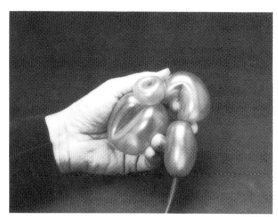

Form a 1 inch loop. Lock twist the two ends of this loop to form the bottom portion of the blossom. The tulip twist should be between the two loops and the uninflated end of the balloon should point to the rear of the blossom.

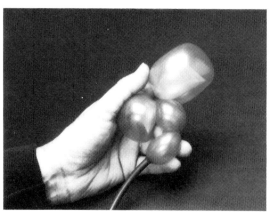

Form a 1 inch bubble behind the blossom. Pinch twist this bubble to force the uninflated end of the balloon downward to form the stem.

SUNFLOWER

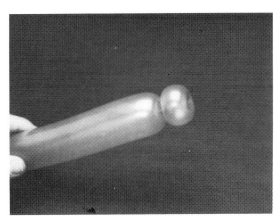

Inflate the balloon leaving a 6 inch uninflated end and tie a knot. Hold the balloon in your left hand with the uninflated end pointing to your left. Form a 1 inch tulip twist at the knot end of the balloon.

Hold the balloon in your left hand with the uninflated end pointing to your right. Form a 2 inch loop. Lock twist the two ends of this loop at the base of the tulip twist.

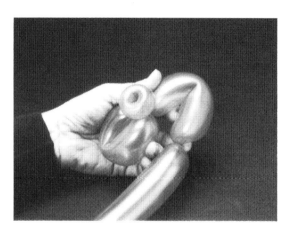

Form a second 2 inch loop. Lock twist the two ends of this loop at the base of the tulip twist opposite the first loop.

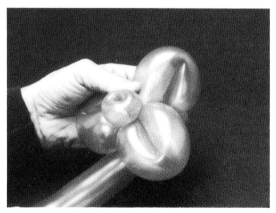

Form a third 2 inch loop. Lock twist the two ends of this loop at the base of the tulip twist. Wedge this loop between the first and second loops.

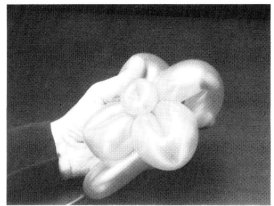

Form a fourth 2 inch loop. Lock twist the two ends of this loop at the base of the tulip twist. Wedge this loop between the first and second loops opposite the third loop.

Form a 1 inch bubble behind the blossom just formed.

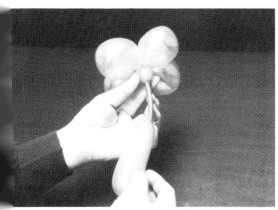

Force the remaining air in the inflated portion of the balloon all the way to the uninflated end. This leaves a slender section of the balloon between the 1 inch bubble and the stem to allow the blossom to move gracefully.

PARROT IN A SWING

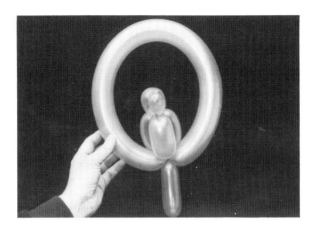

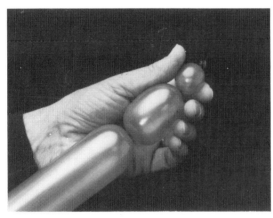

Inflate the balloon leaving a ½ inch uninflated end and tie a knot. Hold the balloon in your left hand with the uninflated end pointing to your right. Form a ½ inch bubble followed by a 1½ inch bubble.

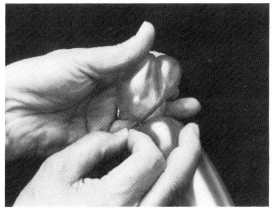

Grasp the knot end of the balloon with your right hand and stretch it back over the 1½ inch bubble. Hold the knot and the twist at the base of the 1½ inch bubble together with your right hand.

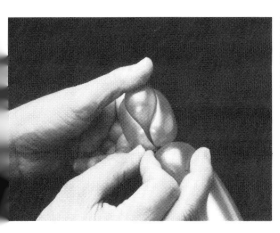

Lock twist the knot and the base of the 1½ inch bubble together by twisting the two bubbles several times with your left hand.

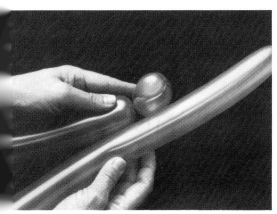

Bring the uninflated end of the balloon along side of the head so that it extends approximately 6 inches above the head. Lock twist the end section of the balloon and the head together at the base of the head.

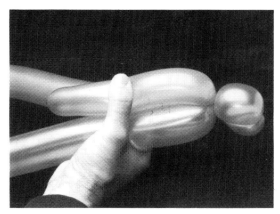

Bring the end section of the balloon and the two sides of the loop together and hold them with your right hand.

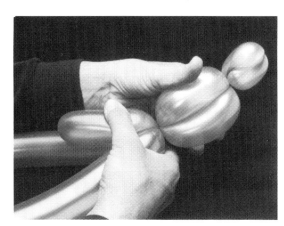

Lock twist these three sections of the balloon together at the middle of the end section of the balloon to form the body and the tail of the parrot.

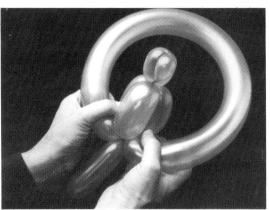

Wedge the body between the two ends of the loop to hold the body inside of the loop leaving the tail hanging down.

LOVE BIRDS

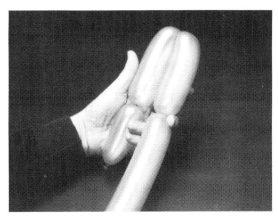

Inflate the balloon leaving a 2 inch uninflated end and tie a knot. Hold the balloon in your left hand with the uninflated end pointing to your right. Form a 3 inch bubble followed by two 4 inch bubbles. Lock twist the two 4 inch bubbles at the base to form the body of the first love bird.

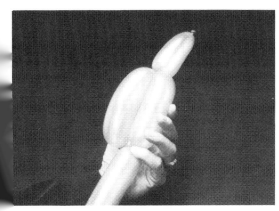

Form a 4 inch bubble and hold it alongside the two 4 inch bubbles.

Roll the two 4 inch bubbles over the single 4 inch bubble with the single 4 inch bubble passing between the two 4 inch bubbles to complete the body of the first love bird.

Form a 1 inch bubble for the head followed by a 1 inch bubble for the head of the second love bird.

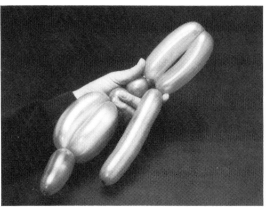

Form two 4 inch bubbles. Lock twist these two bubbles at the base to form the body of the second love bird.

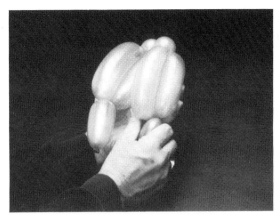

Form a 4 inch bubble and hold it alongside the two 4 inch bubbles.

Roll the two 4 inch bubbles over the single 4 inch bubble with the single 4 inch bubble passing between the two 4 inch bubbles to complete the body of the second love bird.

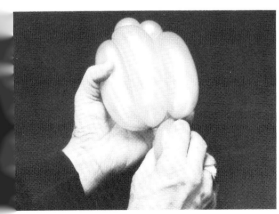

Lock twist the 3 inch bubble formed in Step 1 and the remaining portion of the balloon at the base of the bodies to form the tails and complete the figure.

LOVE BIRDS IN A SWING

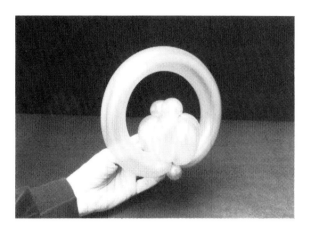

Inflate the balloon all the way. Allow a fairly large amount of air to escape to soften the balloon and tie a knot. Form a ½ inch bubble followed by two 1 ½ inch bubbles. Lock twist the two 1 ½ inch bubbles at the base to form the body of the first love bird.

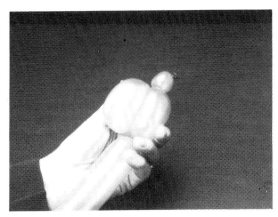

Form a 1½ inch bubble and hold it alongside the two 1½ inch bubbles.

Roll the two 1½ inch bubbles over the single 1½ inch bubble with the single 1½ inch bubble passing between the two 1½ inch bubbles to complete the body of the first love bird.

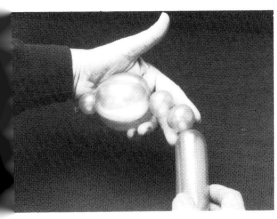

Form a ¾ inch bubble for the head followed by a ¾ inch bubble for the head of the second love bird.

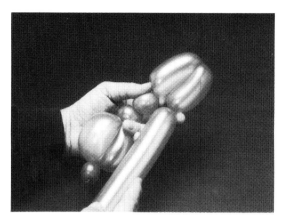

Form two 1½ inch bubbles. Lock twist these two bubbles at the base to form the body of the second love bird.

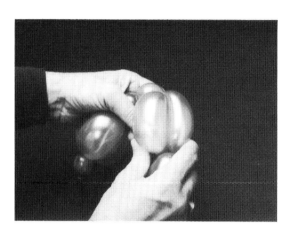

Form a 1½ inch bubble and hold it alongside the two 1½ inch bubbles.

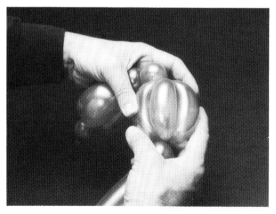

Roll the two 1½ inch bubbles over the single 1½ inch bubble with the single 1½ inch bubble passing between the two 1½ inch bubbles to complete the body of the second love bird.

Lock twist the ½ inch bubble formed in Step 1 and the remaining portion of the balloon to hold the base of the two love birds together.

Form a ½ inch bubble at the end of the remaining portion of the balloon. Form a loop around the two love birds with the remaining portion of the balloon so that one love bird is on each side of the loop. Lock twist the two ½ inch bubbles to form the tails and complete the figure.

SWAN

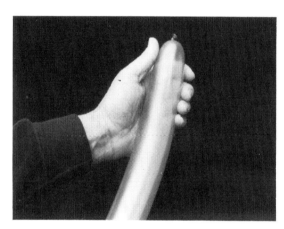

Inflate the balloon leaving a 3 inch uninflated end and tie a knot. Hold the balloon in your left hand with the uninflated end extending downward.

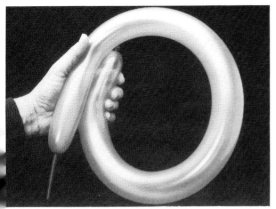

Bring the uninflated end of the balloon up and around to form a loop with the two ends of the balloon overlapping approximately 6 inches.

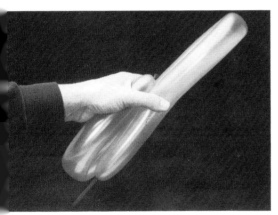

Bring the outer portion of the loop in alongside the overlapped ends of the balloon so that the knot end is approximately in the middle of the doube loop which is formed and the uninflated end extends just beyond the lower portion of the double loop.

Lock twist the three sections of the balloon together at the middle of the double loop making sure the knot is locked in at the twist.

Tuck one side of the double loop up through the other side of the double loop to form the body and tail.

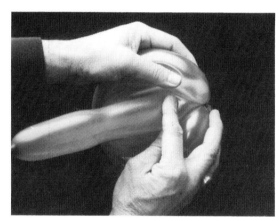

Wedge the base of the uninflated portion of the balloon between the ends of the outer loop to form the neck and to hold it upright.

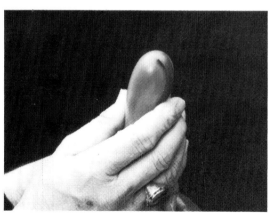

Fold the uninflated tip of the balloon down along the front of the neck and hold it at the very tip with the first finger of your right hand.

Grasp the neck with both hands and squeeze it, forcing the air into the uninflated tip to form the head.

EAGLE

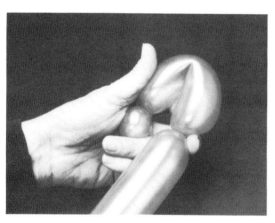

Inflate the balloon leaving a 6 inch uninflated end and tie a knot. Hold the balloon in your left hand with the uninflated end pointing to your right. Form a 1 inch bubble followed by a 1½ inch loop. Lock twist the two ends of this loop to form the tail.

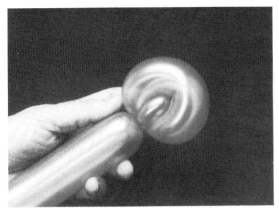

Tuck the 1 inch bubble inside the 1½ inch loop to complete the tail.

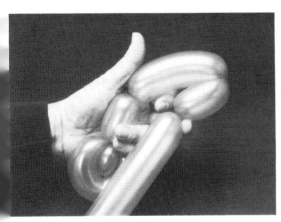

Form a 2 inch bubble for the body followed by a 4 inch bubble and a 2 inch bubble. Lock twist the 4 inch bubble and the 2 inch bubble at the base to form one wing.

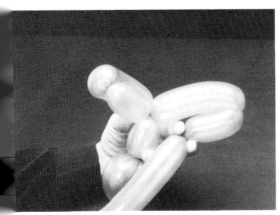

Form a 4 inch bubble and a 2 inch bubble. Lock twist these two bubbles at the base to form the other wing.

Form a 1 inch bubble followed by three ½ inch bubbles and another 1 inch bubble. Lock twist the two 1 inch bubbles at the base to form the legs.

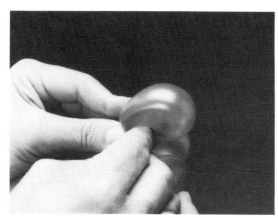

Hold the uninflated tip of the balloon down alongside the portion of the balloon which forms the neck with your finger. Squeeze the neck with both hands until the air is forced into the uninflated tip to form the head and beak.

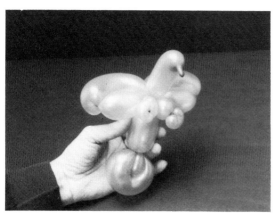

Pinch twist the first and third ½ inch bubbles of the leg assembly to form the feet. Pop the second ½ inch bubble to separate the legs and complete the figure.

TURKEY

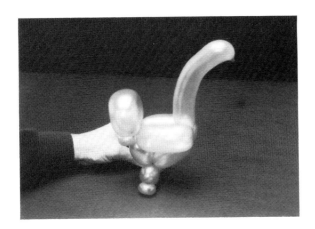

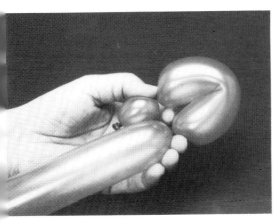

Inflate the balloon leaving a 6 inch uninflated end and tie a knot. Hold the balloon in your left hand with the uninflated end pointing to your right. Form a 1 inch bubble followed by a 2 inch loop.

Lock twist the two ends of this loop to form the tail. Tuck the 1 inch bubble inside the 2 inch loop to complete the tail.

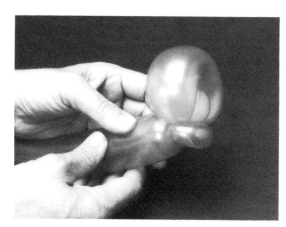

Form a 1 inch bubble. Pinch twist this bubble at the base of the tail to hold the tail upright.

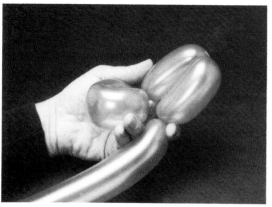

Form two 3 inch bubbles. Lock twist these two 3 inch bubbles at the base to form the body.

Form a 1 ½ inch bubble followed by a 1 inch bubble, three ½ inch bubbles, and another 1 inch bubble. Lock twist the two 1 inch bubbles at the base to form the legs.

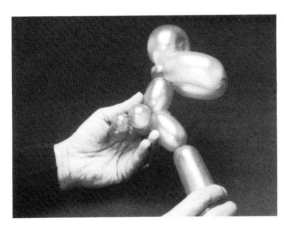

Form a 1 ½ inch bubble.

Wedge the end of this 1½ inch bubble and the base of the remaining portion of the balloon between the ends of the two 3 inch bubbles which were formed in Step 4 to complete the body and to hold the neck upright.

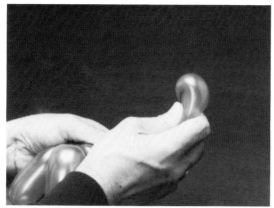

Hold the tip of the uninflated portion of the balloon down alongside the portion of the balloon which forms the neck with your finger. Squeeze the neck with both hands until the air is forced into the uninflated tip to form the head and beak.

Pinch twist the first and third ½ inch bubbles of the leg assembly.

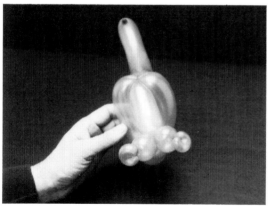

Pop the second ½ inch bubble to separate the legs and complete the figure.

ROAD RUNNER

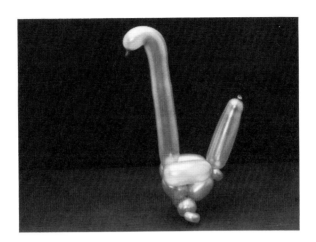

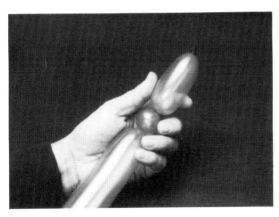

Inflate the balloon leaving a 6 inch uninflated end and tie a knot. Hold the balloon in your left hand with the uninflated end pointing to your right. Form a 2½ inch bubble for the tail followed by a ¾ inch bubble.

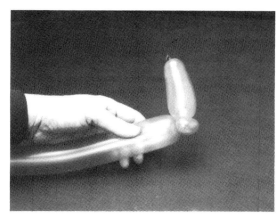

Pinch twist the ¾ inch bubble to hold the tail upright.

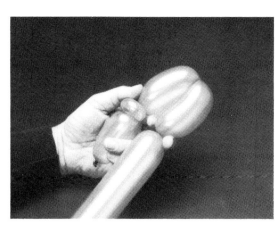

Form two 2½ inch bubbles. Lock twist these two bubbles at the base to form the body.

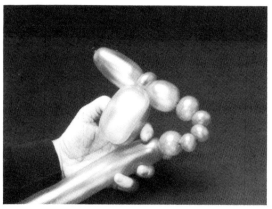

Form a 1 inch bubble followed by a 1 inch bubble, three ½ inch bubbles, and another 1 inch bubble. Lock twist the second and third 1 inch bubbles at the base to form the legs.

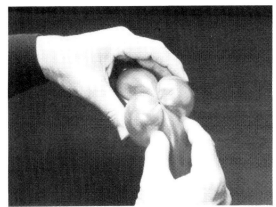

Form a 1 inch bubble. Wedge this 1 inch bubble and the base of the remaining portion of the balloon between the ends of the two 2½ inch bubbles formed in Step 3 to complete the body and hold the neck upright.

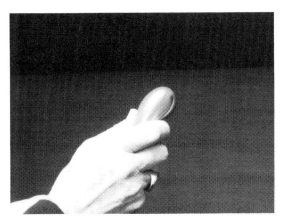

Hold the uninflated tip of the balloon down alongside the portion of the balloon which forms the neck with your finger. Squeeze the neck with both hands until the air is forced into the uninflated tip to form the head and beak.

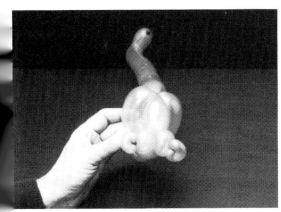

Pinch twist the first and third ½ inch bubbles of the leg assembly to form the feet. Pop the second ½ inch bubble to separate the legs and complete the figure.

TURTLE

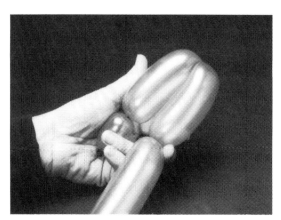

Inflate the balloon leaving a 4 inch uninflated end and tie a knot. Hold the balloon in your left hand with the uninflated end pointing to your right. Form a 1 inch bubble for the head followed by two 4 inch bubbles. Lock twist the two 4 inch bubbles at the base.

Form a 4 inch bubble. Hold this 4 inch bubble against the two 4 inch bubbles formed in Step 1.

Roll the two 4 inch bubbles over the single 4 inch bubble with the single 4 inch bubble passing through between the two 4 inch bubbles to complete the body.

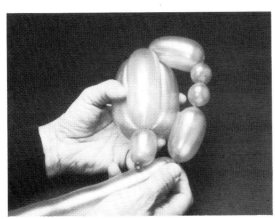

Form a 2 inch bubble followed by two ½ inch bubbles and another 2 inch bubble. Lock twist the base of the last 2 inch bubble around the base of the head to complete the legs on one side.

Form a 2 inch bubble followed by two ½ inch bubbles and another 2 inch bubble. Lock twist the remaining portion of the balloon around the point where the body and the back legs join to form the legs on the other side and complete the figure. The uninflated tip of the balloon becomes the tail.

ALLIGATOR

Inflate the balloon leaving a 6 inch uninflated end and tie a knot. Hold the balloon in your left hand with the uninflated end pointing to your right. Form a 3 inch bubble for the head followed by a 1 inch bubble.

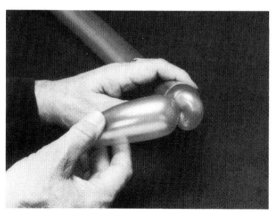

Pinch twist this 1 inch bubble.

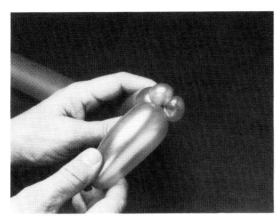

Twist the pinch twisted bubble in half twisting each half three or four times to form the eyes.

Form a 1 inch bubble for the neck followed by a 1 inch bubble, three ½ inch bubbles, and another 1 inch bubble. Lock twist the second and third 1 inch bubbles at the base to form the front legs.

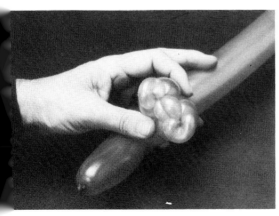

Pinch twist the first and third ½ inch bubbles twisting each at least four times. Pop the second ½ inch bubble to separate the front legs.

Form a 5 inch bubble for the body followed by a 1 inch bubble, three ½ inch bubbles, and another 1 inch bubble. Lock twist the two 1 inch bubbles at the base to form the back legs.

Pinch twist the first and third ½ inch bubbles twisting each at least four times. Pop the second ½ inch bubble to separate the back legs and complete the figure.

FROG

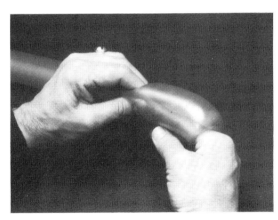

Inflate the balloon leaving an 8 inch uninflated end and tie a knot. Hold the balloon in your left hand with the uninflated end pointing to your left. Form a 3 inch tulip twist at the knot end of the balloon.

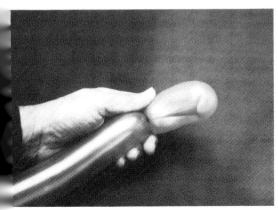

Leave this tulip twist offset as illustrated.

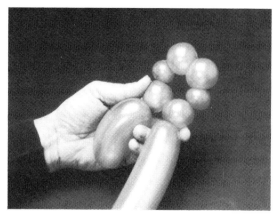

Form a 1 inch bubble, a ¾ inch bubble, two 1 inch bubbles, a ¾ inch bubble, and another 1 inch bubble. Lock twist the first and fourth 1 inch bubbles at the base to form a six bubble loop.

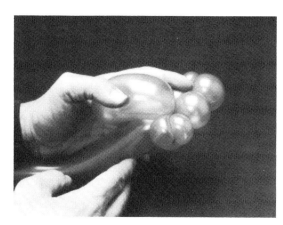

Lock twist the first 1 inch bubble and the first ¾ inch bubble at the base to form one back leg.

Lock twist the fourth 1 inch bubble and the second ¾ inch bubble at the base, twisting them at least four times, to form the other back leg.

Form a small bubble at the end of the 3 inch tulip twist twisting it at least four times.

Twist this small bubble in half twisting each half three or four times to form the eyes.

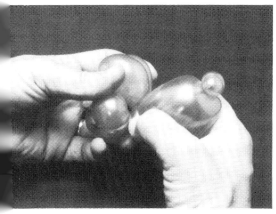

Position the body over the front legs with the eyes on top of the body to complete the figure. Remove the remaining inflated portion of the balloon by popping it.

BULLFROG

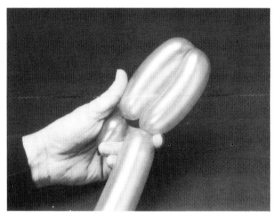

Inflate the balloon leaving an 8 inch uninflated end and tie a knot. Hold the balloon in your left hand with the uninflated end pointing to your right. Form a 1 inch bubble for the head followed by two 3 inch bubbles. Lock twist the two 2 inch bubbles at the base to form the body.

Form a 1 inch bubble followed by a ½ inch bubble, a ¾ inch bubble, three ½ inch bubbles, a ¾ inch bubble, a ½ inch bubble and another 1 inch bubble. Lock twist the two 1 inch bubbles at the base to form a nine bubble loop for the front leg assembly.

Pinch twist the first and fifth ½ inch bubbles to form the joints in the front legs.

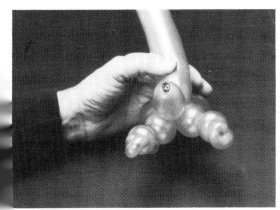

Pinch twist the second and fourth ½ inch bubbles twisting each at least four times. Pop the third ½ inch bubble to separate the front legs.

Form a ¾ inch bubble at the base of the head. Pinch twist this bubble. Twist the pinch twisted bubble in half twisting each half three or four times to form the eyes.

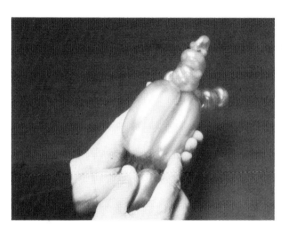

Form a 3 inch bubble. Hold it alongside and beneath the two 3 inch bubbles which form the body.

Roll the two 3 inch bubbles down over the single 3 inch bubble with the single 3 inch bubble passing between the two 3 inch bubbles to complete the body.

Form a 1½ inch bubble followed by a ½ inch bubble, a 1 inch bubble, three ½ inch bubbles, a 1 inch bubble, a ½ inch bubble, and another 1½ inch bubble. Lock twist the two 1½ inch bubbles at the base to form a nine bubble loop for the back leg assembly.

Pinch twist the first and fifth ½ inch bubbles to form the joints in the back legs.

Pinch twist the second and fourth ½ inch bubbles twisting each at least four times. Pop the third ½ inch bubble to separate the back legs. The uninflated tip of the balloon becomes the tail.

FISH

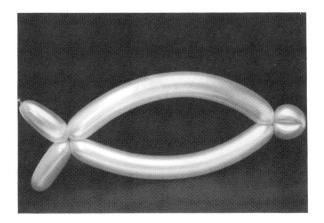

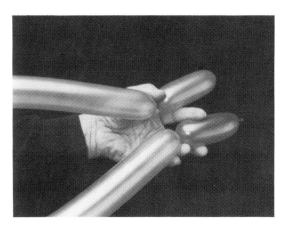

Inflate the balloon all the way. Allow a small amount of air to escape from the balloon to soften it and tie a knot. Form a 3 inch bubble at each end of the balloon.

Lock twist these two bubbles at the base to form the tail fins.

Pinch the balloon to form a 2 inch loop at a point opposite the tail fins. Lock twist the ends of this loop to form the mouth.

KISSING FISH

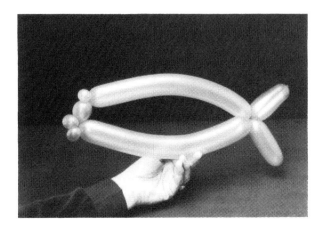

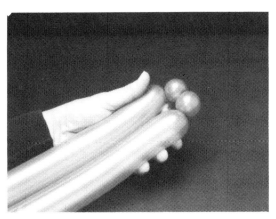

Inflate the balloon all the way. Allow a fairly large amount of air to escape from the balloon to soften it, and tie a knot. Twist the balloon at the middle and form two 1 inch bubbles on one side of the twist.

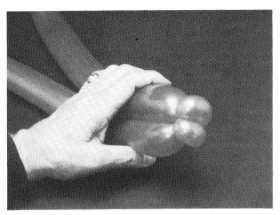

Pinch twist these two 1 inch bubbles to form the mouth.

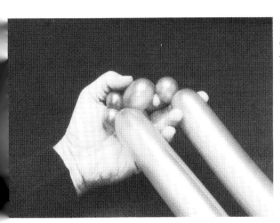

Form a 1 inch bubble on the opposite side of the original twist followed by a ½ inch bubble.

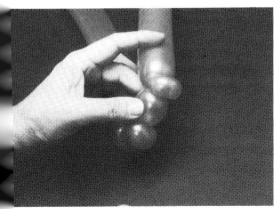

Pinch twist the ½ inch bubble.

Twist the pinch twisted bubble in half twisting each half three or four times to form the eyes.

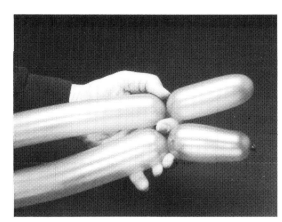

Form a 3 inch bubble at each end of the balloon. Lock twist these two bubbles at the base to form the tail fins and complete the figure.

Figures other than animals can easily be formed using the same basic twists that have been explained and used thus far.

HEADPHONES

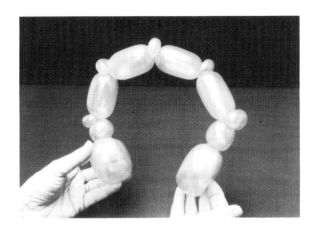

Inflate the balloon leaving a 6 inch uninflated end and tie a knot. Hold the balloon in your left hand with the uninflated end pointing to your right. Form a 1 inch bubble followed by a 1½ inch loop. Lock twist the two ends of this loop to form an ear piece.

Tuck the 1 inch bubble inside the 1½ inch loop to complete the ear piece.

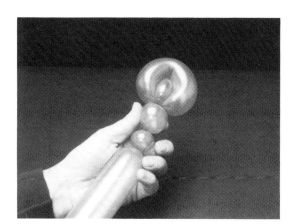

Form a 1 inch bubble followed by a ½ inch bubble. Pinch twist this ½ inch bubble to give shape to the head piece.

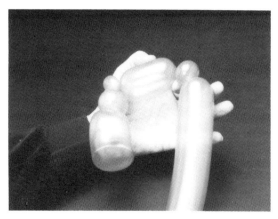

Form a 2 inch bubble followed by a ½ inch bubble. Pinch twist this ½ inch bubble to give shape to the head piece.

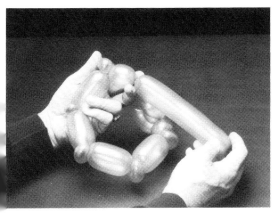

Continue forming 2 inch bubbles followed by ½ inch pinch twists until approximately 5 inches of inflated balloon remain.

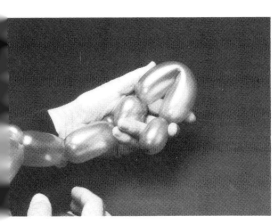

Form a 1 inch bubble followed by a 1½ inch loop. Lock twist the two ends of this loop to form the second ear piece.

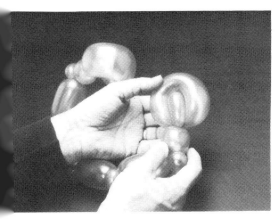

Tuck the remaining end of the balloon inside the 1½ inch loop to complete the ear piece.

PISTOL

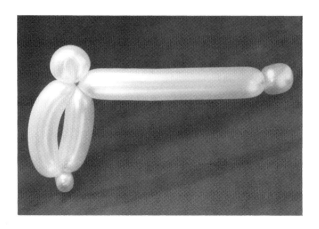

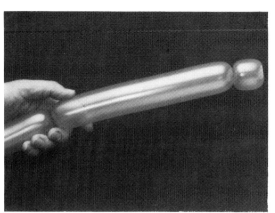

Inflate the balloon leaving a 6 inch uninflated end and tie a knot. Hold the balloon in your left hand with the uninflated end pointing to your left. Form a 1 inch tulip twist at the knot end of the balloon followed by an 8 inch bubble.

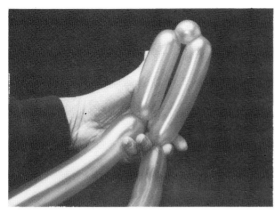

Hold the 8 inch bubble in your left hand with the uninflated end of the balloon pointing to your right. Form a 4 inch bubble, a 1 inch bubble, and a 5 inch bubble. Lock twist the 4 inch bubble and the 5 inch bubble at the base to form the hand grip. Make sure the 5 inch bubble ends up at the rear of the hand grip.

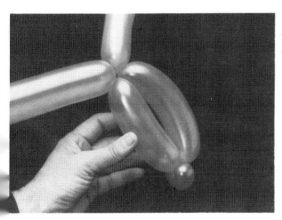

Pinch twist the 1 inch bubble at the end of the hand grip, twisting it at least five times.

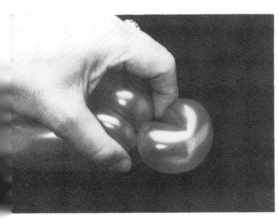

Form a 1 inch loop at the point where the hand grip and the barrel join. Lock twist the ends of this loop to form the hammer, twisting it at least five times. Remove the remainder of the inflated portion of the balloon by popping it.

The pistol can be fired twice by squeezing the hand grip hard enough to pop the two bubbles that form the hand grip.

SWORD/LIGHT SABRE

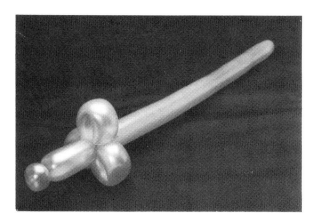

Inflate the balloon leaving a 2 inch uninflated end and tie a knot. Hold the balloon in your left hand with the uninflated end of the balloon pointing to your left. Form a 1 inch tulip twist at the knot end of the balloon.

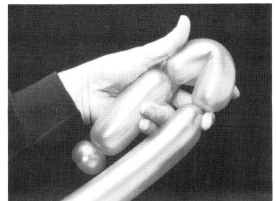

Hold the balloon in your left hand with the uninflated end of the balloon pointing to your right. Form a 4 inch bubble for the handle followed by a 2 inch loop. Lock twist the ends of this loop to form the first section of the hand guard.

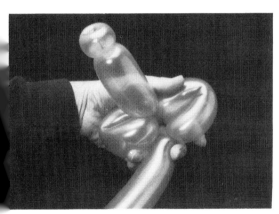

Form a second 2 inch loop. Lock twist the ends of this loop to form the second section of the hand guard.

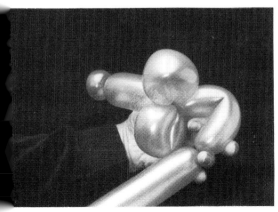

Form a third 2 inch loop. Lock twist the ends of this loop to complete the hand guard.

SKI POLE

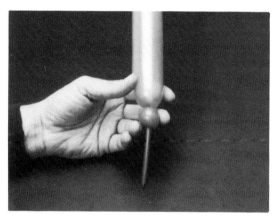

Inflate the balloon leaving a 3 inch uninflated end. Allow a small amount of air to escape from the balloon before tying the knot. Hold the balloon in your left hand with the uninflated end pointing to your right. Form a ½ inch bubble next to the uninflated tip of the balloon.

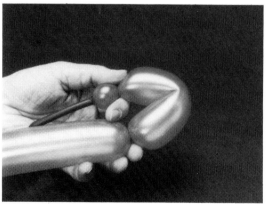

Form a 2 inch loop. Lock twist the two ends of this loop to form the first section of the basket.

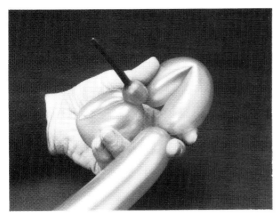

Form a second 2 inch loop. Lock twist the two ends of this loop to form the second section of the basket.

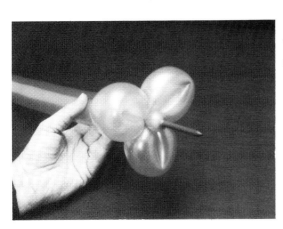

Form a third 2 inch loop. Lock twist the two ends of this loop to complete the basket.

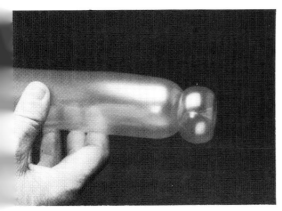

Form a 1 inch tulip twist at the knot end of the balloon to complete the figure.

SKATEBOARD

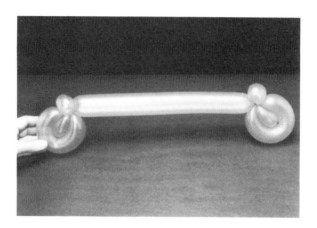

Inflate the balloon leaving a 4 inch uninflated end and tie a knot. Hold the balloon in your left hand with the uninflated end pointing to your right. Form a 1 inch bubble followed by a 2 inch loop. Lock twist the two ends of this loop to form one wheel.

Tuck the 1 inch bubble inside the 2 inch loop to complete one wheel.

Form a 1 inch bubble. Pinch twist this bubble to hold the wheel in the proper position.

Form a 12 inch bubble for the board followed by a 2 inch loop. Lock twist the two ends of this loop to form the other wheel.

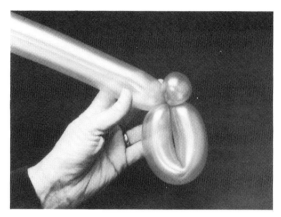

Form a 1 inch bubble. Pinch twist this bubble to hold the wheel in the proper position.

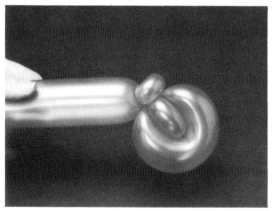

Tuck the remaining end of the balloon inside the 2 inch loop to form the second wheel and complete the figure.

SCOOTER

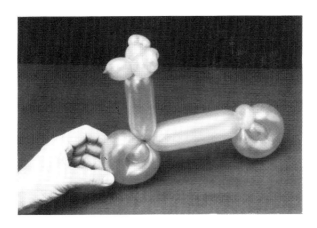

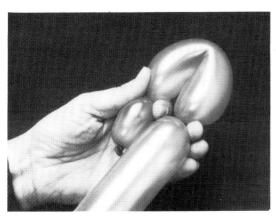

Inflate the balloon leaving a 6 inch uninflated end and tie a knot. Hold the balloon in your left hand with the uninflated end pointing to your right. Form a 1 inch bubble followed by a 2 inch loop. Lock twist the two ends of this loop to form the rear wheel.

Tuck the 1 inch bubble inside the 2 inch loop to complete the rear wheel.

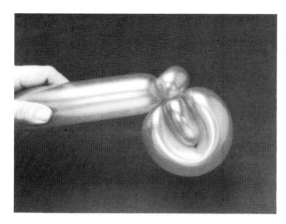

Form a 1 inch bubble. Pinch twist this bubble to hold the wheel in the proper position.

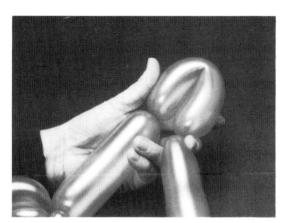

Form a 5 inch bubble for the board followed by a 2 inch loop. Lock twist the two ends of this loop to form the front wheel.

Form a 1 inch bubble. Pinch twist this bubble at the point where the board and the front wheel join.

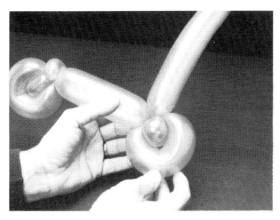

Tuck this pinch twisted bubble inside the 2 inch loop to complete the front wheel.

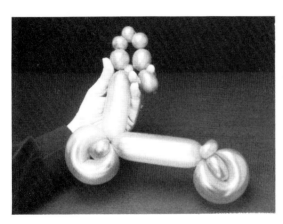

Form a 4 inch bubble for the upright followed by a 1 inch bubble, three ½ inch bubbles, and another 1 inch bubble. Lock twist the two 1 inch bubbles at the base to form the handlebars.

Pinch twist the first and third ½ inch bubbles twisting each at least four times. Pop the second ½ inch bubble to separate the handlebars and complete the figure.

CHOPPER

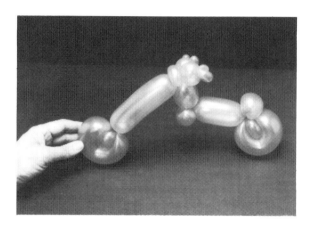

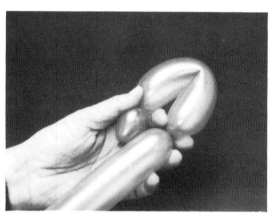

Inflate the balloon leaving a 6 inch uninflated end and tie a knot. Hold the balloon in your left hand with the uninflated end pointing to your right. Form a 1 inch bubble followed by a 2 inch loop. Lock twist the two ends of this loop to form the rear wheel.

Tuck the 1 inch bubble inside the 2 inch loop to complete the rear wheel.

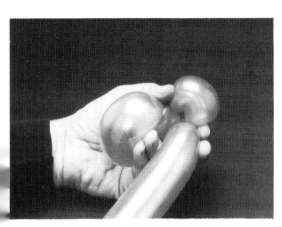

Form a 1 inch loop for the seat back.

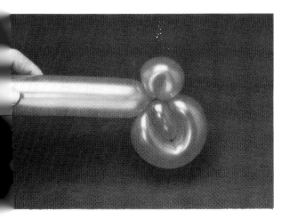

Lock twist the two ends of this loop to complete the seat and to hold the rear wheel in the proper position.

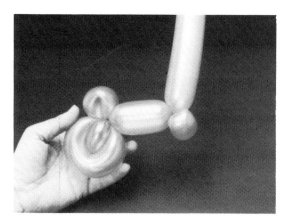

Form a 3 inch bubble for the frame followed by a 1½ inch bubble. Pinch twist this 1½ inch bubble to form the motor.

Form a 2 inch bubble for the upright followed by a 1 inch bubble, three ½ inch bubbles, and another 1 inch bubble. Lock twist the two 1 inch bubbles at the base to form the handlebars.

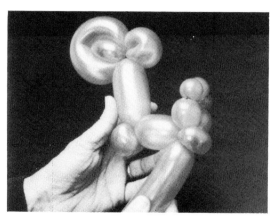

Form a 1 inch bubble. Pinch twist this bubble in front of the handlebars to hold them in the proper position.

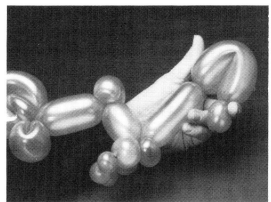

Form a 3 inch bubble for the front forks followed by a 2 inch loop. Lock twist the two ends of this loop to form the front wheel. Tuck the remaining end of the balloon inside the 2 inch loop to complete the front wheel.

Pinch twist the first and third ½ inch bubbles of the handlebar assembly twisting each at least four times. Pop the second ½ inch bubble to separate the handlebars and complete the figure.

BICYCLE

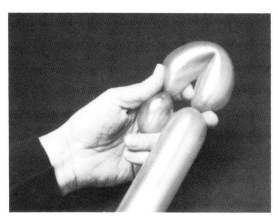

Inflate the balloon leaving a 6 inch uninflated end and tie a knot. Hold the balloon in your left hand with the uninflated end pointing to your right. Form a 1 inch bubble followed by a 2 inch loop. Lock twist the two ends of this loop to form the rear wheel.

Tuck the 1 inch bubble inside the 2 inch loop to complete the rear wheel.

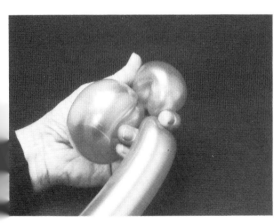

Form a 1 inch loop for the seat back.

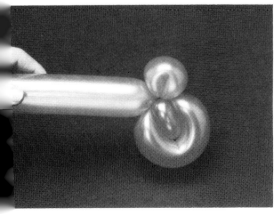

Lock twist the two ends of this loop to complete the seat and to hold the rear wheel in the proper position.

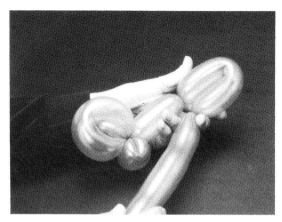

Form a 3 inch bubble for the frame followed by a 2 inch loop. Lock twist the two ends of this loop to form the front wheel.

Form a 1½ inch bubble for the upright followed by a 1 inch bubble, three ½ inch bubbles, and another 1 inch bubble. Lock twist the two 1 inch bubbles at the base to form the handlebars.

Form a 1 inch bubble. Pinch twist this bubble in front of the handlebars to hold them in the proper position.

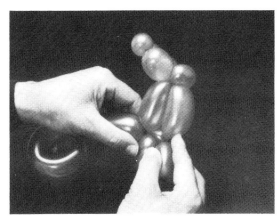

Form a 2 inch bubble to complete the upright.

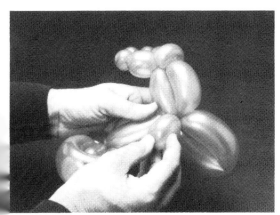

Lock twist the base of this bubble around the base of the upright at the point where the front wheel and the upright join. Tuck the remaining portion of the balloon inside the 2 inch loop to complete the front wheel.

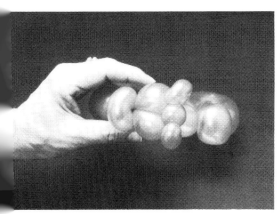

Pinch twist the first and third ½ inch bubbles of the handlebar assembly twisting each at least four times. Pop the second ½ inch bubble to separate the handlebars and complete the figure.

AIRPLANE

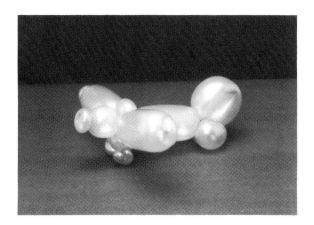

Inflate the balloon leaving a 6 inch uninflated end and tie a knot. Hold the balloon in your left hand with the uninflated end pointing to your left. Form a ½ inch tulip twist at the knot end for the propeller.

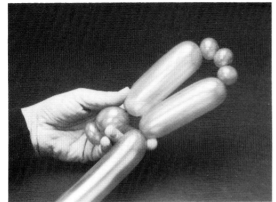

Hold the balloon in your left hand with the uninflated end pointing to your right. Form a 1 inch bubble followed by a 4 inch bubble, three ½ inch bubbles, and another four inch bubble. Lock twist the two 4 inch bubbles at the base to form the wings.

Form a 1 inch bubble followed by three ½ inch bubbles and another 1 inch bubble. Lock twist the two 1 inch bubbles at the base to form the landing gear.

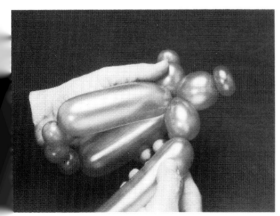

Form a 1 inch bubble for the cockpit.

Pinch twist this bubble to complete the cockpit.

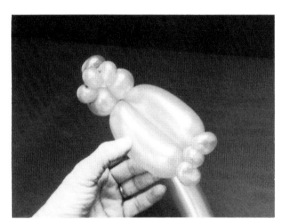

Pinch twist the first and third ½ inch bubbles of the wing assembly twisting each at least four times. Pop the second ½ inch bubble to separate the wings. Place the cockpit crossways between the wings to hold them in the proper position.

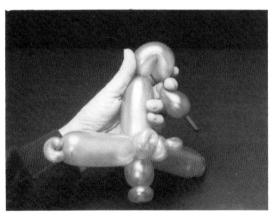

Form a 3 inch bubble for the body followed by a 2 inch loop. Lock twist the two ends of this loop to form the rudder.

Form a 1 inch loop. Lock twist the two ends of this loop to form one elevator.

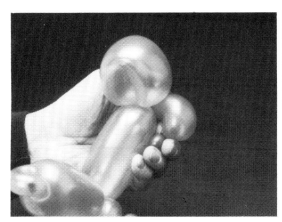

Form a second 1 inch loop. Lock twist the two ends of this loop twisting it at least four times to form the other elevator. Remove the remaining portion of the balloon by popping it.

Pinch twist the first and third ½ inch bubbles of the landing gear assembly twisting each at least four times. Pop the second ½ inch bubble to separate the landing gear and complete the figure.

JET

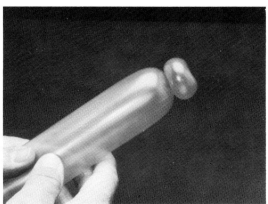

Inflate the balloon leaving an 8 inch uninflated end and tie a knot. Hold the balloon in your left hand with the uninflated end pointing to your left. Form a ½ inch tulip twist at the knot end for the exhaust port.

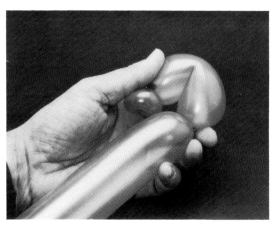

Form a 1½ inch loop. Lock twist the two ends of this loop to form the rudder.

Form a 1 inch bubble followed by three ½ inch bubbles and another 1 inch bubble. Lock twist the two 1 inch bubbles at the base to form the elevators.

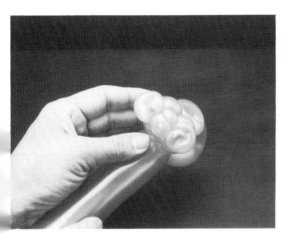

Pinch twist the first and third ½ inch bubbles twisting each at least four times.

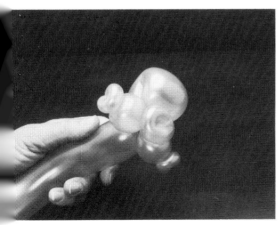

Pop the second ½ inch bubble to separate the elevators and complete the tail section.

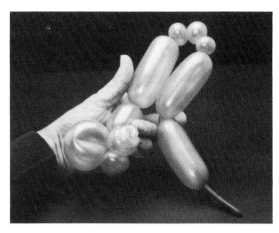

Form a 3 inch bubble for the body followed by a 3 inch bubble, three ½ inch bubbles, and another 3 inch bubble. Lock twist the second and third 3 inch bubbles at the base to form the wings.

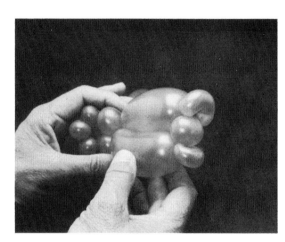

Pinch twist the first and third ½ inch bubbles twisting each at least four times.

Form a 1 inch bubble at the base of the wings followed by three ½ inch bubbles and another 1 inch bubble. Lock twist the two 1 inch bubbles at the base to form the landing gear.

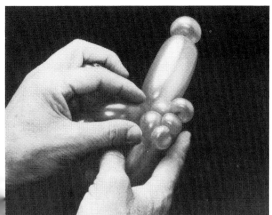

Pinch twist the first and third ½ inch bubbles twisting each at least four times. Pop the second ½ inch bubble of the wing assembly to separate the wings. Pop the second ½ inch bubble of the landing gear assembly to separate the landing gear.

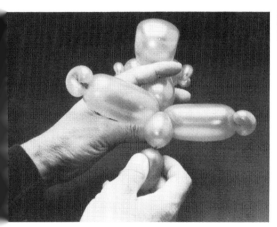

Form a 1 inch bubble for the cockpit.

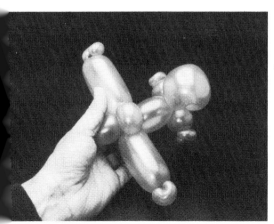

Pinch twist this bubble and position it between the wings to complete the cockpit and to hold the wings level.

BI-PLANE

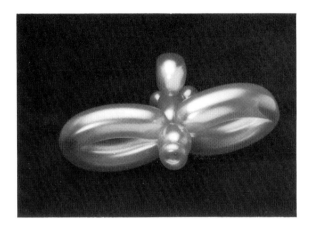

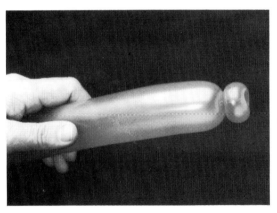

Inflate the balloon leaving a 6 inch uninflated end and tie a knot. Hold the balloon in your left hand with the uninflated end pointing to your left. Form a ½ inch tulip twist at the knot end of the balloon for the propeller.

Hold the tulip twist in your left hand with the uninflated end pointing to your right. Form a 1 inch bubble for the fuselage followed by a 5 inch loop. Lock twist the ends of this loop to form the wings on one side.

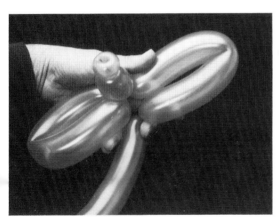

Form a second 5 inch loop. Lock twist the ends of this loop to form the wings on the other side.

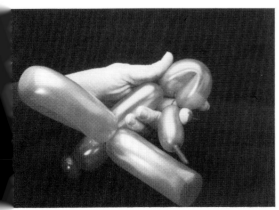

Form a 3 inch bubble for the body followed by a 2 inch loop. Lock twist the ends of this loop to form the rudder.

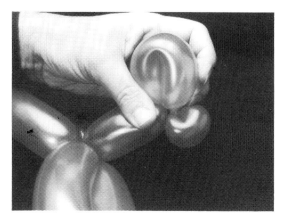

Form a 1 inch loop. Lock twist the ends of this loop to form one elevator.

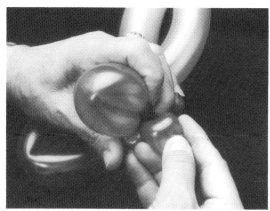

Form a second 1 inch loop. Lock twist the ends of this loop, twisting it at least five times, to form the other elevator. Remove the remaining portion of the uninflated end of the balloon by popping it.

HELICOPTER

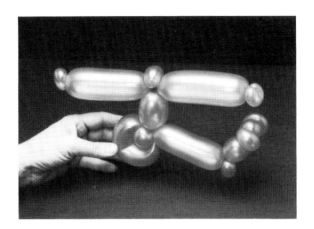

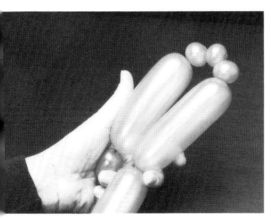

Inflate the balloon leaving a 6 inch uninflated end and tie a knot. Hold the balloon in your left hand with the uninflated end pointing to your right. Form a 1 inch bubble followed by a 4 inch bubble, three ½ inch bubbles, and another 4 inch bubble. Lock twist the two 4 inch bubbles at the base to form the rotary wings.

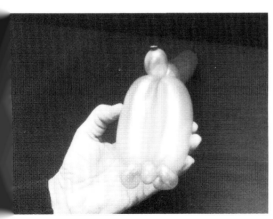

Pinch twist the first and third ½ inch bubbles twisting each at least four times. Pop the second ½ inch bubble to separate the rotary wings.

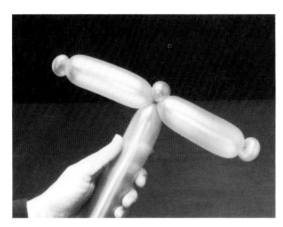

Pinch twist the 1 inch bubble at the knot end of the balloon and position it between the rotary wings to hold them in place.

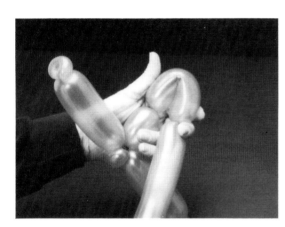

Form a 2 inch bubble for the upright followed by a 2 inch loop. Lock twist the two ends of this loop to form the cockpit.

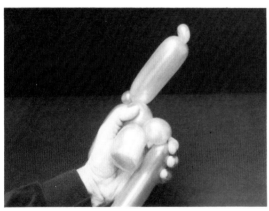

Form a 1 inch bubble. Pinch twist this bubble and tuck it inside the 2 inch loop to complete the cockpit.

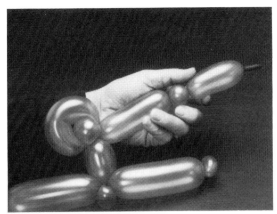

Form a 4 inch bubble for the tail followed by a 1 inch bubble.

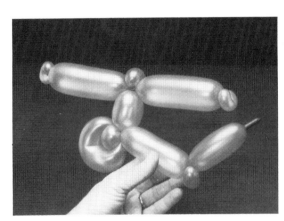

Pinch twist the 1 inch bubble to angle the end of the tail section upwards.

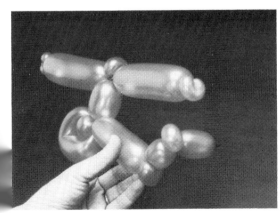

Form a 1 inch bubble for the upright portion of the tail section followed by a 1 inch bubble. Pinch twist this last 1 inch bubble to form the stabilizer propeller and complete the figure.

SNOOPY

Inflate the balloon leaving an 8 inch uninflated end and tie a knot. Hold the balloon in your left hand with the uninflated end pointing to your right. Form an "S" shape in your left hand with approximately 6 inches of the inflated portion of the balloon.

Squeeze a small amount of air out of this portion of the balloon and twist the balloon at the end of the ''S.''

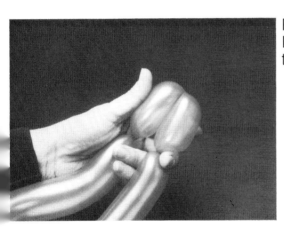

Form two 1½ inch bubbles. Lock twist these two bubbles at the base to form the ears.

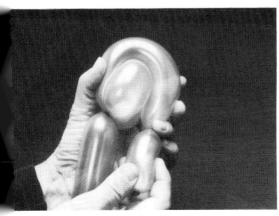

Form a 1½ inch bubble at the knot end of the balloon. Wrap the remaining portion of the ''S'' around the two 1½ inch bubbles formed in the previous step. Lock twist the single 1½ inch bubble around the base of the two 1½ inch bubbles to complete the head.

Form a 1 inch bubble for the neck followed by two 1½ inch bubbles. Lock twist the two 1½ inch bubbles at the base to form the front legs.

Form a 2 inch bubble for the body followed by two 1½ inch bubbles. Lock twist the two 1½ inch bubbles at the base to form the back legs. Be sure to leave a small bubble of air at the base of the tail to hold the back legs in place.

WOODSTOCK

Inflate the balloon leaving a 6 inch uninflated end and tie a knot. Hold the balloon in your left hand with the uninflated end pointing to your right. Form a 1 inch bubble for the beak followed by a chain of seven ½ inch bubbles.

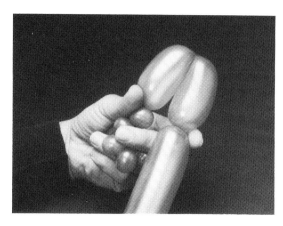

Form two 1½ inch bubbles at the end of the seven bubble chain. Lock twist these two bubbles at the base.

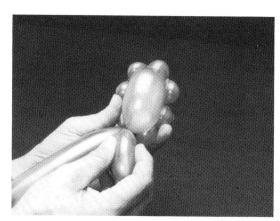

Wrap the seven bubble chain around the two 1½ inch bubbles. Lock twist the 1 inch bubble at the knot end of the balloon around the base of the two 1½ inch bubbles to form the beak and complete the head.

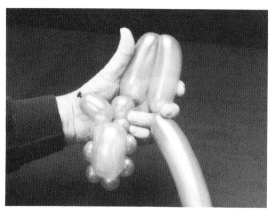

Form a 1 inch bubble for the neck followed by two 3 inch bubbles for the body.

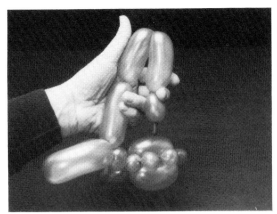

Form a 3 inch bubble followed by two 2 inch bubbles. Lock twist the two 2 inch bubbles at the base to form the legs.

Hold the single 3 inch bubble alongside the two 3 inch bubbles formed in the previous step.

Roll the two 3 inch bubbles over the single 3 inch bubble with the single 3 inch bubble passing between the two 3 inch bubbles to complete the figure.

DOLL

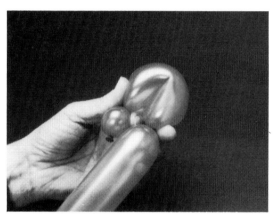

Inflate the balloon leaving an 8 inch uninflated end and tie a knot. Hold the balloon in your left hand with the uninflated end pointing to your right. Form a ¾ inch bubble followed by a 1½ inch loop. Lock twist the two ends of this loop.

Tuck the ¾ inch bubble inside the 1½ inch loop to complete the head.

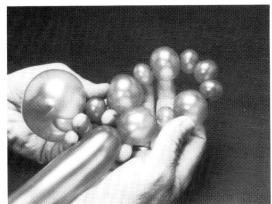

Form a ½ inch bubble for the neck followed by a 1 inch bubble, a ½ inch bubble, a 1 inch bubble, three ½ inch bubbles, a 1 inch bubble, a ½ inch bubble, and a 1 inch bubble. Lock twist the first and fourth 1 inch bubbles at the base to form a 9 bubble loop.

Pinch twist the first and fifth ½ inch bubbles to form the elbows.

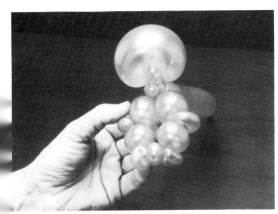

Pinch twist the second and fourth ½ inch bubbles twisting each at least four times to form the hands.

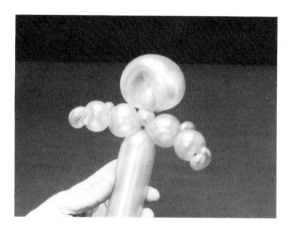

Pop the third ½ inch bubble to separate the arms.

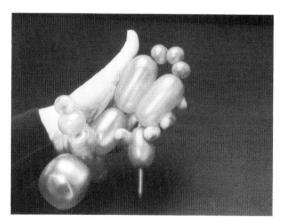

Form a 1½ inch bubble for the body followed by a 2 inch bubble, three ½ inch bubbles, and another 2 inch bubble. Lock twist the two 2 inch bubbles at the base to form the legs.

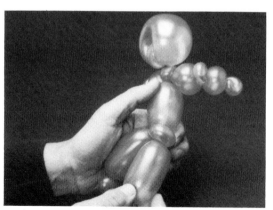

Form a ½ inch bubble. Pinch twist this bubble to form one hip.

Form a second ½ inch bubble. Pinch twist this bubble twisting it at least four times to form the other hip. Remove the remaining portion of the balloon by popping it.

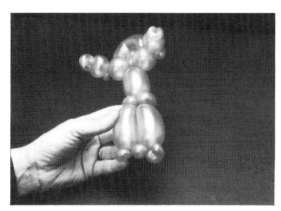

Pinch twist the first and third ½ inch bubbles of the leg assembly to form the feet. Pop the second ½ inch bubble to separate the legs and complete the figure.

SAINT BERNARD

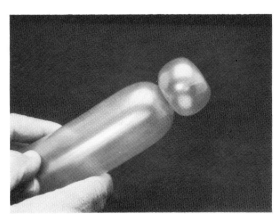

Inflate the balloon leaving a 6 inch uninflated end and tie a knot. Hold the balloon in your left hand with the uninflated end pointing to your left. Form a 1 inch tulip twist at the knot end of the balloon.

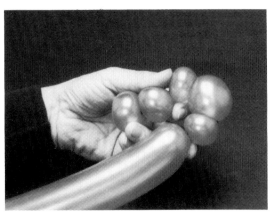

Hold the balloon in your left hand with the uninflated end pointing to your right. Form a 1 inch bubble, a ¾ inch bubble, a 1½ inch bubble, and another ¾ inch bubble. Lock twist the two ¾ inch bubbles at the base to form the head.

Pinch twist the two ¾ inch bubbles to form the ears and complete the head.

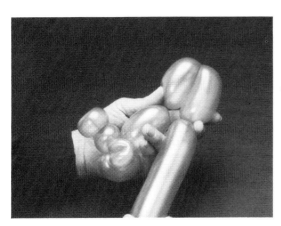

Form a 1½ inch bubble for the neck followed by two 1½ inch bubbles. Lock twist these two 1½ inch bubbles at the base to form the front legs.

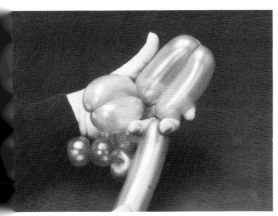

Form two 3 inch bubbles. Lock twist these two bubbles at the base to form the body.

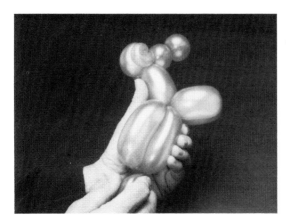

Form a 3 inch bubble and hold it alongside the two 3 inch bubbles.

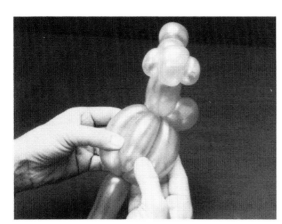

Roll the two 3 inch bubbles over the single 3 inch bubble with the single 3 inch bubble passing between the two 3 inch bubbles to complete the body.

Form two 1½ inch bubbles. Lock twist these two bubbles at the base to form the back legs.

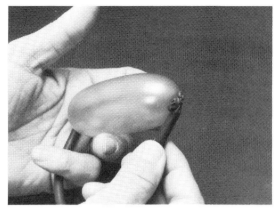

Take a second balloon and inflate it to form a 2 inch bubble and tie a knot. Tie the tip of the uninflated end of the balloon and the knot end of the balloon together.

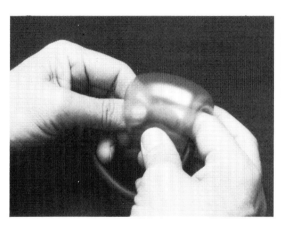

Tuck the knot that is formed through the inflated portion of the balloon and form a tulip twist with the uninflated portion of the balloon forming a loop.

Place this loop over the head of the figure to represent a brandy (root beer) keg.

There are a number of detailed figures that can be formed that must begin with an uninflated portion at each end of the balloon. The trunk of the elephant, the tail of the unicorn, and the kickstand of the motorcycle, for instance, are each formed at the uninflated lip end of the balloon.

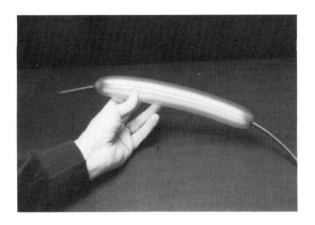

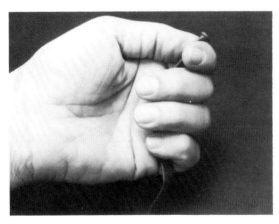

Hold a portion of the balloon inside of your hand to prevent it from expanding while inflating the balloon.

ELEPHANT

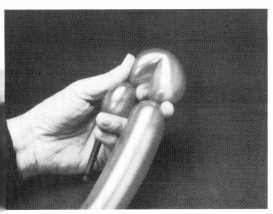

Inflate the balloon keeping 3 inches of the balloon uninflated at the lip end and leaving 4 inches uninflated at the opposite end and tie a knot. Form a 1 inch bubble next to the uninflated portion of the balloon at the lip end followed by a 1½ inch loop. Lock twist the two ends of this loop to form one ear.

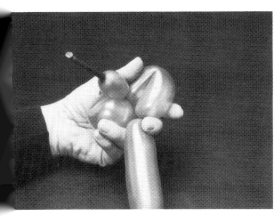

Form a 1½ inch loop. Lock twist the two ends of this loop to form the other ear.

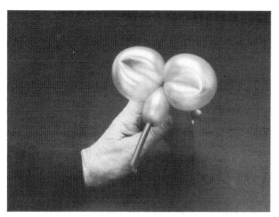

Position the head and trunk between the ears as illustrated.

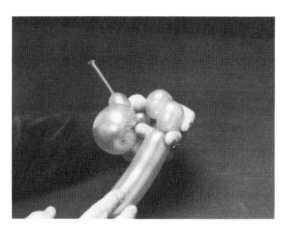

Form a 1 inch bubble for the neck followed by two 1 inch bubbles. Lock twist these two 1 inch bubbles at the base to form the front legs.

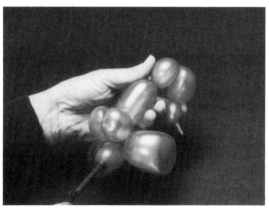

Form a 2 inch bubble for the body followed by two 1 inch bubbles. Lock twist the two 1 inch bubbles at the base to form the back legs. Be sure to leave a small bubble of air at the base of the tail to hold the back legs in place.

UNICORN

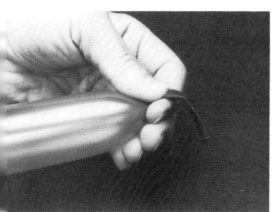

Inflate the balloon keeping 1 inch of the balloon uninflated at the lip end and leaving 6 inches uninflated at the opposite end. Tie the knot next to the inflated portion of the balloon at the lip end.

Form a ½ inch bubble next to the knot followed by two 1½ inch bubbles. Lock twist the two 1½ inch bubbles at the base to form the back legs.

Form a 1½ inch bubble for the body followed by two 1½ inch bubbles. Lock twist the last two 1½ inch bubbles at the base to form the front legs.

Form a chain of six ½ inch bubbles. Lock twist the first and sixth ½ inch bubbles at the base to form a six bubble loop.

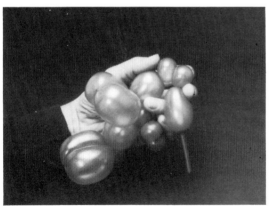

Form a 1½ inch bubble for the neck followed by two ½ inch bubbles. Lock twist the two ½ inch bubbles at the base to form the ears.

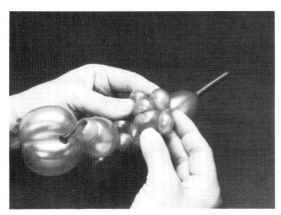

Stretch the 6 bubble loop over the ears wedging the ears between the third and fourth ½ inch bubbles to form the mane.

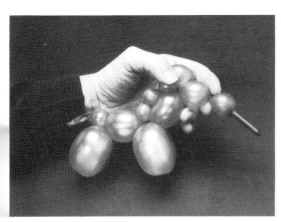

Twist the remaining inflated portion of the balloon in half.

Tie the uninflated tip of the balloon around the last twist to form the horn and complete the figure.

MOTORCYCLE WITH A KICK STAND

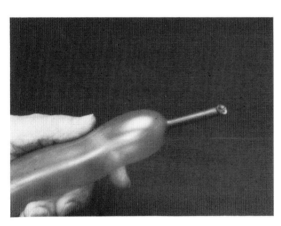

Inflate the balloon keeping 2 inches of the balloon uninflated at the lip end and leaving 6 inches uninflated at the opposite end and tie a knot.

Form a ½ inch bubble next to the uninflated lip end of the balloon followed by a 1½ inch loop. Lock twist the two ends of this loop to form the back wheel.

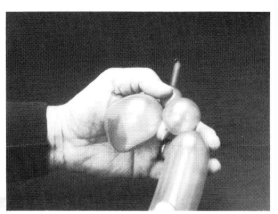

Form a 1 inch bubble.

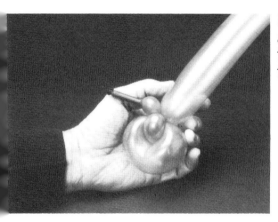

Pinch twist this 1 inch bubble and tuck it inside the center of the 1½ inch loop to complete the back wheel.

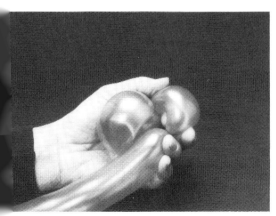

Form a 1 inch loop. Lock twist the two ends of this loop to form the seat and to hold the rear wheel in position. Make sure the uninflated lip end is on the left side of the rear wheel.

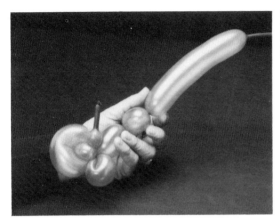

Form a 1½ inch bubble for the frame followed by a 1 inch bubble.

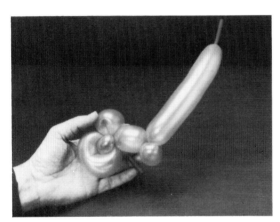

Pinch twist the 1 inch bubble to form the motor.

Form a 1 inch bubble for the upright followed by a ¾ inch bubble, three ½ inch bubbles and another ¾ inch bubble. Lock twist the two ¾ inch bubbles at the base to form the handlebars.

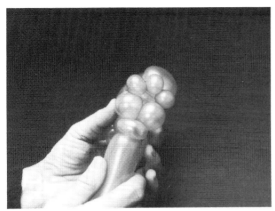

Form a 1 inch bubble. Pinch twist this bubble in front of the handlebars to hold them in the proper position.

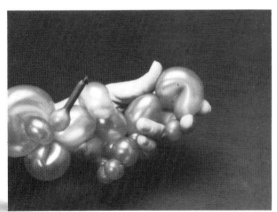

Form a 2 inch bubble for the front forks followed by a 1½ inch loop. Lock twist the two ends of this loop to form the front wheel. Tuck the remaining portion of the balloon inside the center of the 1½ inch loop to complete the front wheel.

Pinch twist the first and third ½ inch bubbles of the handlebar assembly, twisting each at least four times. Pop the second ½ inch bubble to separate the handlebars and complete the figure.

BALLOON ART

For information on ordering *Balloon Art* products,
call Toll-Free 1-800-453-1356.
In Utah call collect (801) 562-5481.

- *Balloon Magic* — Paperback Edition
- *Balloon Art* — Hardback Edition
- *Deluxe Balloon Art Video Cassette* — 60-Minute VHS or Beta
- *Deluxe Balloon Magic Kit* — Includes Instruction Book, Pump and Balloons
- *Package of 144 Pencil Balloons*
- *Marlin Balloon Pump*

10% for shipping and handling will be charged to all orders.
Please allow four to six weeks for delivery.